1ˢᵗ edition released May 2014. 2ⁿᵈ edition released May 2017.

This information has been channelled for learning purposes and giving information for instruction.

Spacing in this book has been purposely done for greater understanding and learning to help the mind comprehend the vast amount of learning within the publication.

The author is not responsible for errors or omissions, does not claim to be qualified to offer legal, professional or medical advice with readers.

Sovereign Lord Emmanuel The Great, Caeayaron (Kryon), the Archangels and Ascended Beings, and the Pleiadians have requested that people purchase legitimate copies only from Caeayaron Ltd as this book has been given to mankind to support peace and love and the Great Divine Purpose.

They will give rays of healings and awakening to all those who are open to greater love and understanding and who support the Great Divine Purpose. They cannot support and give rays of love and awakening to anyone who has not received a legitimate copy purchased from Caeayaron Ltd

To contact Caeayaron Ltd: E-mail: caeayaron@gmail.com

Home page: www.caeayaron.com

Join Suzanna Maria Emmanuel on Facebook & youtube

ISBN 978-1-912214-00-6

Your History Revealed

How You Are Involved

Halisarius, Pleiadian Chief Commander

speaks to mankind

By Suzanna Maria Emmanuel

,timonials from Readers

I had been reading books for over 50 years, always hoping that the next book I read would answer all my questions and put all the pieces of the jig-saw puzzle together.

As I began to read Suzanna's first book, a voice seemed to whisper very softly and so gently in my ear, "A Komo Ha Halima." I have heard this phrase many times – it is the greeting that Pleiadians use every time Suzanna channels one of them. I had the distinct feeling a Pleiadian was with me and would be with me as I read the words of Halisarius.

Halisarius's teaching regarding human history and mankind's ultimate destiny, was for me, so unique, so profound and so humbling. It moved me greatly, and deep within me, it has changed me forever.

Thank you Suzanna and thank you Halisarius for answering all my questions and putting all the pieces of the jig-saw puzzle together for me.

Graham Jones, New Zealand, Star Sacred World Healer, activated by Caeayaron

Before this, a more exciting, enlightening, and important book did not exist. My heart and my being just buzzed feeling the truth resonating within me. Wow! There is information about our star family, goodies and baddies, our history, the darkness, the Galactic Federation of Light and our greater purpose in being here. That knowledge alone strengthened my heart with love and gave me a profound sense of peace within. This is a book written by a very highly evolved being of great love, a being who is here, to help humanity to grow into love and bring peace to our earth. An out of this world read from the higher dimensions of love and light flows, a must read for all truth seekers.

Jacqui Hanson, New Zealand, Star Sacred World Healer, activated by Caeayaron

This is a beautifully written, easy to read, simple to understand book, containing many powerful insights into a journey that we are unable to remember, but when reading it is one that feels very real and familiar.

Many 'aha' moments will leave you feeling lighter, more empowered and more at peace with this life.

If anyone is truly searching for answers, then I believe that reading this book may just be the beginning of a deeper understanding, taking you on a new journey of 'self-discovery' of who you are and a new truth that will enhance your life, far beyond any explanation given to you until now.

Halisarius reveals information never before given to mankind. It was such a privilege to have been one of the first to read this. A new and increasing respect for my life occurred when I turned each page.

This is a wonderful comprehensive introduction into a new reality and an important understanding for all. This book allows you to discover more about yourself, mankind, earth and the universe, which we live in. Fear of the unknown is gently removed leaving the reader deeply satisfied and open to greater expansion of thought. The greatest gift is the development of a new 'inner truth' of who you are and your place on this earth.

Thank you Suzanna for bringing to us all this wonderful gift, Namaste, Sharan Collier-Caskey, New Zealand, Star Sacred World Healer, activated by Caeayaron

When I received Halisarius's book I was filled with so much excitement. Everything that was written resonated with me, I couldn't stop reading it. I was filled with so much joy and gratitude.

I had so many questions answered and it all made so much sense. I just wanted to shout it to everyone, "Here are the answers to so many questions." I felt this strong knowing for Halisarius and a great love for him. It was almost overwhelming. Thank you. Thank you Halisarius for you awakened me, and I remembered you.

Namaste, soooo much love to all, Linda Jensen, New Zealand, Star Sacred World Healer, activated by Caeayaron

What an amazing book to help humanity understand more of who they are on all levels. This book is easy to read and understand for anyone at any stage of their spiritual awakening. I would highly recommend this read to anyone who desires to understand why we humans suffer pain, disease, sickness, fear, anger, and what we can do about it. It explains the game of life we are playing in on earth and how we are controlled by it.

It explains how we can claim our power back and use our brains to a higher capacity. The incredible power of forgiveness is explained deeply in a way I now understand completely! A deep realization I got from this book is that we do have choice in this life and each and every one of us can change our lives into more peaceful, abundant, healthy, loving joyful ones when we wake up to who we are.

Finally an ancient history of earth that actually makes sense from the times of Atlantis & Lemuria!!

Much love and deep gratitude Suzanna for your devotion to channeling this beautiful book and to Halisarius for coming through with this knowledge to help humanity awaken.

Namaste, Donna Richmond, New Zealand, Star Sacred World Healer, activated by Caeayaron

Dedication

I, Suzanna Maria Emmanuel, thank Halisarius, Chief Commander of the Pleiadians, Great Leader of the Galactic Federation of Light for never giving up on us as humans. Thank you, Halisarius, for loving us enough to bring through your teachings and guiding us upwards. Thank you for not giving up on the people.

I dedicate this book to the greatest love in the universe to bring all universes back to love and peace so that love and peace can eternally exist, bringing all creation upwards into greater strength, love and harmonic flows collectively.

I dedicate this book to Caeayaron, Master of Magnetic Forces, Flows & Alignment, Sovereign Lord Emmanuel The Great, The Sacred White Brotherhood, The Galactic Federations of Light, the Universal Love Body, and all who in Divine Will work hard towards the Great Alignment when all will become with One Purpose, that being of great love.

I dedicate this book to the Blue Star Universes and the Red Star Universes, for the fight for the Light has been hard for many billions of years.

I dedicate this book to my close friends who are supporting the Divine Mission. I love you always. I dedicate this book to all lovers of love and truth who are working along with Divine to bring love and peace to this plane.

Namaste, love, light and angel hugs, Suzanna Maria Emmanuel♥♥

Contents

Introduction by Suzanna Maria Emmanuel

'Namaste, I see the Divine in you as you see the Divine in me.' I always say this to everyone who comes to me to hear Divine speaking. 'Isn't this the most beautiful way to greet each other? For in these spaces, as you see Divine within me, you see Divine within you, and you begin to recognize Divinity in you as we all have Divine within us.'

In January 2014, Halisarius approached me and asked me to write a book with him. For two weeks I sat with him as he began to bring through many teachings, many of them, at that time, were foreign to me.

I did not know, at the time of writing with Halisarius, that Caeayaron would approach me at the end of April 2014. I did not know about the greater game of the universe, or my great role in Ancient Lemuria as the Divine Love Element Light Grid Programmer. All that information was still to be revealed to me.

When I was asked by Caeayaron, late 2016, to go through the book once again so that it could be released with a fresh format, I was surprised to read the teachings once more, for now I understood so much more as so much has since been revealed, and all the teachings of Halisarius made sense in all ways. I was truly amazed and thanked Halisarius even more as my spiritual appreciation had greatly deepened.

This book is filled with many, many treasures. It is filled with Pleiadian wisdom which lovers of love and truth will thoroughly enjoy. It is filled with answers we have been seeking for so long.

The teachings of Halisarius are a perfect way to begin to understand the spiritual journey. It gives a deep insight in relatively easy lessons. The lessons are short, easy to understand and leave us to ponder upon the deeper meanings.

As a channel of Divine Love, I appreciate Divine Truth so very much as all truths resonate deep within me. It is a part of me. I speak on behalf of many people who love truth as truth also resonates with the lovers of love.

Here, at this time, we are being shown the way to the greater love consciousness, to grow as one, to grow as one beautiful people with one purpose, and that is to become of LOVE, to grow as LOVE, to open to the power of LOVE.

We are learning to work as One Great Love Family with Star Beings, and this is why Halisarius has brought this book to us, as lovers of love and truth, because of his great love and his great dedication to us as people and to the Great Universe.

Throughout these pages you will feel the great love of the Pleiadians with you. They are beautiful beings of great love and they have great love for you and can help you with all aspects of your life. We only need to open our hearts to receive their great love and wisdom.

We are truly blessed when we allow them to be a part of our Light Team who are eternally guiding us to our Greater Soul Journey.

Namaste, much love, light and eternal blessings from Divine Love,

Suzanna Maria Emmanuel♥♥

About Suzanna Maria Emmanuel

Suzanna Maria Emmanuel is the designated channel for Sovereign Lord Emmanuel The Great. She is the Ascension channel, designated by Divine Love, to bring millions of people back to the greater love, guided by Divine.

Suzanna is the Light Grid Programmer and Divine Love Element of Caeayaron (Kryon). Caeayaron activates people who come to the Divine Pineal Gland Activations, connecting them back into their Sacred Light Lemurian Codes for their great healings and the great ascension. Suzanna works with Halisarius and Ammorah, from the Pleiadian Realms, who are here to guide people towards the Great Love Consciousness.

A Komo Ha Halima

Greetings, I AM Halisarius,

Pleiadian Chief Commander & Chief Leader,

Great Leader of the Galactic Federation of Light Society.

Part 1: Introduction by the Pleiadians

We are from the realms of the Pleiades. We are here to help you understand yourselves better. You are going through shifts and stirrings as all of mankind is awakening to their greater side, their greater self.

You are in a time period that was prophesied many thousands of years ago. In our time zone, this seems to us as only yesterday. However, please understand that we are in a different time zone than you are. Your time is different to ours and all other existence.

You seem to think time is stable and fundamental to your growth. You seem to think your clocks are stable. Yet, in all reality, your time is nothing but a speck of time in the universal bodies of light.

This book has been especially channeled down to a beautiful trance channel, we call our Blue Star. A long time ago, we made an arrangement with the Great Sacred White Brotherhood to bring information to the earth when it was needed, only through an Angel who would come here from the highest of vibrations. This one would be our channel and our divine Blue Star.

Why is this important? It is because as you read through this book you will unravel the greatest mysteries in your history. You may like to relook at your book you call the Bible after reading this book from us, the Pleiadians in light. You will come across many new teachings to help you awaken to light within you.

You are in a time that many of your Leaders do not desire to have on your plane, as when you understand these light awakening teachings, your whole way of life will change. That we promise to you.

We greet you and we are your teachers and we desire to help you understand us, as we desire to help you understand yourselves.

Greetings, I AM Halisarius, Pleiadian Chief Commander.

We Pleiadians are your Family of Light

We Pleiadians,

are your Family of Light.

We are here to guide you,

to higher ways of life,

to higher ways of evolution,

to higher ways of consciousness,

to higher ways of understanding,

to help you find your greater power,

within you to create,

a planet of,

divine love,

unity and beauty.

May you feel,

within your hearts,

your greater guidance.

May your blessings,

shine forever,

eternally.

A Komo Ha Halima, Pleiadian Greetings

I greet you with Universal Divine Love.

I greet you with my Sacred Loving Divine Heart.

As I recognize Universal Love within me,

I also recognize it within you,

for we were created with Divine Love Source.

We were created with the Power of the Great Love.

As you recognize the Power of the Great Love within me,

and as I recognize the Power of the Great Love within you,

we stand together in Universal Love,

as Brothers and Sisters.

We stand together as One,

as one Universal Family of Light.

One together,

in the Divine Glory,

of the Great Oneness,

The Great Family of Light.

Opening up a portal of your sacred hearts collectively

Before you can open the portal,

of your Sacred Hearts collectively,

to bring unity to your race,

to bring love to your race,

you must learn to find your love.

When you find your love within,

you will find great power within,

you will find the great keys within.

These are the keys of:

Love,

Greatness,

Knowledge,

Power,

Wisdom,

Healing,

Growth,

Peace.

A Komo Ha Halima

Greetings, I AM Halisarius,
Pleiadian Chief Commander & Chief Leader,
Great Leader of the Galactic Federation of Light Society.

Part 2: Learning to unify in love

How do we greet each other on the Pleiadian Realms? We teach one another how to respect each other and how to love each other and always greet each other with greatness.

This is my teaching at this time. How do you greet yourselves in the morning and how do you greet each other?

Do you wake up with a smile? Do you understand your life? Do you have love for the ones you work with and for your family?

Dear friends, here I will teach you some of the greatest universal secrets in all of the universal light.

Your love for yourselves is about how you view yourself. Everything is a reality to the way you view yourself. A mirror if you like. What you believe your life to be, you will receive in the mirror. The mirror always reflects your beliefs back to you. You are living in a mirror of existence and reflection, constantly mirroring each other with learnings of greatness.

We, as Pleiadian brothers and sisters, your Family of Light, understand these lessons well. Like you, we have not always understood this way of being either until we grew tired and frustrated because our ways were not working. We fought against each other and we could not achieve, though our minds were great, greater than yours at this time.

We came together as a body and discussed these matters. To unite our realms we made decrees and foundations.

One of them was to learn to love who we were and find our fundamental belief system.

We worked on this with difficult processes. We united together and began to see the very secret of all of life. When we worked apart, though intelligent as we were, we could not create unification and brotherhood. When we worked together with one thought, we created, we believed, we united.

This fundamental belief process is your key also to higher evolution.

How do you believe your world to be? For you live in energies of illusion. As time is an illusion for you, your world is also an illusion made up of your belief systems and the way you see your lives to be.

You tend to congregate and flock with those with similar belief structures and then make the reality happen in your life.

You may find this difficult to believe, but please keep reading, for these times are about awakening and finding greater structure for your world.

Hence, you have many challenges in your life happening. You may have many fears together, and because you have forgotten to check your own belief structure, you have become caught up in other people's belief structures and have left your own beliefs behind. This has caused much entanglement on your planet and thus you believe you are powerless.

We desire to help you become untangled in your game of life. We desire to teach you and instruct you in ways to help you become more firm within your own belief structure.

A Komo Ha Halima, Greetings, I AM Halisarius, Pleiadian Leader, and Great Leader of The Galactic Federation of Light.

A Komo Ha Halima

Greetings, I AM Halisarius,

Pleiadian Chief Commander & Chief Leader,

Great Leader of the Galactic Federation of Light Society.

Part 3: Will you open your mind to greater understanding?

We come in peace to you. We wish to help you understand us better so that we can help you understand you better.

I want to discuss the illusion of your reality further.

You have come to an age now where you are more open to new learnings. Your scientists have discovered much.

Only a few hundred years ago, you believed your world to be flat. You had many theories and many scientists in those days to 'prove' to the people who lived back then, that it was so and nothing could change those theories.

However, at times, brave people stepped forward and challenged issues in your society. A brave man sailed the seas desiring to prove these theories of the earth being flat, wrong. He knew in his heart it could not be so and that there was much to be discovered.

We are asking you to be the discoverers.

Are you a discoverer? Or are you a listener to theories, not willing to look outside of your so called 'reality' of your life?

You exist in a world of energies. These energies are not as real as you believe them to be. If I was going to discuss the Greater Plan with you, as I will further into this book as you carry on reading with me, would you be willing to open your mind and look inside of your heart?

You have become entrenched with ideas. As young children, you go to a school system and you are made to believe certain ideas and how the world has been created. You may go to your church and be taught the old book, the Bible, and you believe it to be so.

You have become filled with ideas and fables of your past and your universe. You are relying too much on your scientific expressions, theories and understandings.

We are here to give your mind material to understand different matters. Some of our ideas may rattle you. Our ideas may challenge you. We will challenge your society, the way you live and see your life.

However friends, to advance your life and the way you take your ideas into your future depends on whether you open your mind to greater understanding or not. You are on a cross road. You are on a road that either leads to eternal destruction of your planet, or to a blessed, loving life.

We know your outcome. We trust you will desire to have a greater union within yourselves as you begin to explore yourselves further. You will begin to see your understanding of greater alignment with all of the universal requirements, to help you evolve to a higher way of life.

We ask you now, are you ready to understand greater ways of exploring? Or will you be determined to be disconnected from your life?

This is an important question as we go into the new understandings of where you are at on your timeline in your history.

Greetings, I AM Halisarius, Chief Commander and Leader of the Pleiadians.

We hold the keys to your records

We hold the keys to your records,

of life,

of your creation,

of your history.

May these records,

which have been sealed,

until this time,

be opened now,

to release the treasures,

to release the secrets,

for now you are in the,

Great Restoration,

the times of the Great Return,

to the Great Love.

We call these times,

'The Great Awakening Consciousness.'

A Komo Ha Halima

Greetings, I AM Halisarius,

Pleiadian Chief Commander & Chief Leader,

Great Leader of the Galactic Federation of Light Society.

Part 4: Learning to have unity with each other

I AM Halisarius and I am bringing you news and love from our realms of awakened Pleiadians in the Light.

Here in the realms of our Pleiadian ways we would like to help you understand more about us and yourselves.

We, as star travelers and time jumpers, have often been with you in your past history of growth and education.

You greeted us warmly and we sat with you in your houses. We taught you our views and how the stars connected. You understood the stars and you understood you come from the stars.

Today, I wish to help you understand your relationship with each other. Again, this was a lesson a long time ago for us also as Pleiadians. We learned in order to move beyond our drifting away from each other, we needed to understand our relationship with one another in order to join together.

You also are in a similar time frame. You, in order to move ahead and evolve into higher understandings, need to move together in greater unity.

On our planets, we call this the 'Great Gathering of Thoughts and Minds.'

We see each other as great. We respect each other and we greet each other as we would greet ourselves. We have learned to go beyond our ego and into the unification of the mind.

Hence, when we come together into the one mind and into the greatness, we do not need to speak to each other but we come together with the telepathic mind. We unravel the mysteries and the greatness together, telepathically.

We have discovered much like this. We have discovered the illusion of all, the illusion of the universe. We have discovered how to create portals to travel from one Star Light energy to another. We have learned to jump into time, into the future and into the past.

We are record keepers. We have recorded your history because your history holds keys to who you are. It holds keys to the many mysteries you have and to your 'Creators,' who have created your universe and your earth.

I mentioned earlier in the pages, that you live in an illusion of your reality and that we would give you many ideas to consider. Again, the result of your considerations is yours to have. We give you the knowledge but the way your story ends is your responsibility.

Our responsibility, or part of our responsibility, is to pass the information written in our record books on to you, so that you remember your history, so that you can make the changes to your planet.

This change can only come from the hearts of mankind. It is a change of life and a change of being, for within the change your whole history of how you see your history to be, will be challenged.

Can you face that? Can you open your mind to that challenge? Can you find the answers within these pages that you have been looking for?

Greetings friends, I AM Halisarius, Pleiadian Chief Leader and Guidance Counselor of the Galactic Federations of Light.

A Komo Ha Halima

Greetings, I AM Halisarius,
Pleiadian Chief Commander & Chief Leader,
Great Leader of the Galactic Federation of Light Society.

Part 5: A mission

A long time ago, I, as well as many of my trusted friends, travelled to your plane. We came to you in peace and with many gifts. I, Halisarius, Pleiadian Chief Leader, made a promise. This promise was to help you in the time when we would join again.

We cried as we departed from each other. I was one of the privileged ones to help you find your way. However, we knew we were required to leave you, as your evolution would be a path that you could only discover for yourselves.

What is this path, you may wonder? What game are you involved in? What did we, Pleiadians, do for you? How can you find the answers to your history?

These questions are in the minds of many who are reading these pages. Please understand we are here to unravel your mind. We hold the keys to your deeper understanding and knowledge and we hold the records of your history.

You are not here by accident. You came on a mission, a mission to bring and harmonize the light of your people and your earth.

You came here as star travelers with the greater understanding of all the history issues of the universe.

You are the mirror of all realities. You hold the keys to greater evolution for all planetary beings in existence. You are powerful creators. You are beings of much light. You are beings of much understanding.

Why do you not feel this way? Why are you confused and lost as a race?

This is because you have become separated with your understandings. Your keys of faith, trust and love have been, as it were, thrown into the oceans and you are searching for them.

Where could they be? Where could you find them? How far and deep will you search your oceans for the keys that seemingly have been lost?

Or have they been lost? Perhaps they were never gone. Perhaps they were simply forgotten about. Perhaps you require a key to unlock the past so that your memory will unfold once again.

A Komo Ha Halima, Greetings, I AM Halisarius, Pleiadian Chief Leader and your Friend in the Star Spaces of Love and Light.

The existence of life is great!

The existence of life is great,

beyond your ability to comprehend.

We are all part of a

Sovereign Universal Body,

one body of light,

separated,

yet together,

all discovering,

life together.

You are also part of,

our eternal light family,

of great discovery.

We are here to help you remember,

so that you can join us once again.

A Komo Ha Halima

Greetings, I AM Halisarius,
Pleiadian Chief Commander & Chief Leader,
Great Leader of the Galactic Federation of Light Society.

Part 6: There are others

A Komo Ha Halima. It is with great pleasure that we are transmitting these words through our Blue Star, our faithful channel and transcriber and our secretary. Suzanna has much work to do on this earth plane. She is from our realms also. She is also from the Archangelic Realms of Light and has vowed to be my transcriber as well as the transcriber for Archangels in the highest of rays.

We are happy you have joined us on these pages. For whoever reads these words, will receive a gift from our Pleiadian people. You will receive the gift of a heart opening from the Star Energies of the greater Light Frequencies.

These star energies are our tools for our advancement also, for we learn much in the frequencies of star energies. We see much and our vision opens. Our clarity sharpens and we have a firmer grip on our evolutionary advancement.

Many of your people understand that you are not the only ones in the universal bodies of planetary existences. It is indeed correct. On your planets around you there is thriving life. They also have many lessons to learn. Many of those are supporting your evolution and growth.

You may not see them with your physical eyes, but like we discussed before, are you willing to spread your thought and ways of understanding? Or perhaps will you stay closed as to how you view your reality to be?

If you do not expand your thinking, how will you expand your ways then? For at this time it is vital you expand your understanding if your race is to survive.

Your survival depends on how much you come together with your hearts. You hold an incredible power within you that you do not understand yet. We will discuss this in further parts of this book.

You are much envied by many in the universe because of the sacred gift you hold which you have not yet discovered together.

The way you see with your eyes you have come to believe it to be so. You believe that you are limited and that you live in your reality. You have forgotten to look into the other space frequencies or higher vibrations.

A long time ago, you knew how to sense and feel within these greater energies. You understood them well, and hence, when travelers from other planetary bodies came to visit you, you were open to their learning. Their understanding and evolution was greater than that of mankind at present.

However, during the process of your evolution, you shut down as it were, to your higher gifts and abilities and you fell into the greater belief that you live in this reality and nothing else could live outside your reality.

There are many, many beings on other stars and planets and in other universes. Your discovery of the universe is only a speck in comparison to what is out there. Many star beings have found you and yet others find it difficult to find you as you can be like a needle in a haystack as it were.

However, for the ones who find you and who desire to learn from you, they are greatly enriched with greater understanding as much of their reality is also your reality.

You can understand from this lesson, you have many brothers and sisters on other planets. When you open your mind and come together with a greater heart of love and peace, you will reunite with them. You will reunite and understand many lessons. Will you open your mind to your star brothers and sisters in the Light?

Greetings, I AM Halisarius, Pleiadian Leader and Teacher. I am also a great teacher for many Star Races in the Love and the Light.

To learn about your love is to open your heart

To learn about your love,

is to open your heart,

to your greater love.

To learn about your life,

is to open your mind,

to greatness,

to higher thoughts,

to grander possibilities.

It is in these higher moments,

you begin to realize,

that greater truths,

could be in existence,

and that indeed you could be,

part of greater existence.

Learn to look within,

and you will find your way home.

A Komo Ha Halima

Greetings, I AM Halisarius,
Pleiadian Chief Commander & Chief Leader,
Great Leader of the Galactic Federation of Light Society.

Part 7: It is time to expand your thinking

We wish to help you understand your life better. We wish to help you understand your history; to help you understand your purpose in life.

At this time, I wish to help you understand more about your creation. This has always been one of the greatest questions in your history, has it not?

A great book was written in your past. A book written by many people, in many different versions and much of it has been altered. This does not mean that all is wrong in your Bible for much of it is right. However, many of the stories have been altered for the power and the control of your people.

Why is this difficult to grasp for you? Is it difficult to grasp for you because you have been led to believe that everything you have been told is truth and there is nothing else?

Please remember the scientist and the theologians who said that the earth was flat. Was that not proven wrong? Yet, these people believed it to be.

Hence, it is time to look at your world. Again, we say to you, everything in your world is an illusion. Your time is not as you may think it is. You are able to slow it down and make it fast; it is all to do with the way you relate to your world and how real you believe your world to be.

It is easy for the human to believe in certain so called truths. Your mind is a miracle. It has many different pathways and your brain works as you would use your computer. It stores databases within larger databases and it takes on new data from other sources.

It does not understand the difference between reality and imagination. It likes to believe in certain truths and it trusts what your history says. You like to investigate your history in books and create your own theories and truths based on what you have been told.

This is because the brain has been trained to do so. It has been trained, throughout the many eons, to believe in certain theories and then it continued to learn from those certain theories in existence.

For the mind to begin to understand other theories, it becomes frightening to the person who owns the mind, as the person and the mind will have to find the relationship between the mind and the person once again in a whole different way of understanding.

This can be frightening as you like to think your theories are sound and solid.

Yet, you are finding out new aspects about your world every day. Look how much you have discovered about your sacred bodies. There is much more to discover. You will discover much between the energy, the emotion and the physical in the future. This holds the key to healing yourselves and finding the greater truth within you.

In the future, you will learn to access your own healing power and depend less on other people to tell you what is wrong and where it is wrong. You will become more empowered within yourself. Many people in your world will not like to hear this as industries will collapse over this knowledge of the people.

Again, it is about keeping you limited and not in the knowing, for is it not safer for those ones to keep you in ignorance? Imagine if a race on earth awakened to their inner power? Imagine if your leaders lost their power and control overnight?

These leaders have been in control of your thinking, your being and your doing. These leaders have kept you in the belief that you needed a savior and that you are sinners. These leaders have led you to believe you are limited and they made you feel safe.

The reality is you have power within you, and once it is unleashed your leaders will no longer be able to keep you limited. You will expand into your greatness! You will bring change to your world!

The great 'reality' of all this is far from their theories and desires. You are far more in power than you believe yourselves to be. I encourage you to think about all these matters and then please return to these lessons to learn more.

Greetings, I AM Halisarius, Pleiadian Leader. I AM in Chief Command for our people.

A Komo Ha Halima

Greetings, I AM Halisarius,

Pleiadian Chief Commander & Chief Leader,

Great Leader of the Galactic Federation of Light Society.

Part 8: Learn to expand who you are with positivity

We wish to say hello to our fellow brothers and sisters on earth. One day, we will reunite once again with you and share with you our stories of the stars and how we are star travelers and we will create much love on your planet with our frequencies of light.

It is a privilege to help you at this time, to help you understand who you are.

You may be asking, why I am giving you short and brief lessons with a little information and then closing the lesson?

We, as Pleiadians, are showing the way for higher growth and higher consciousness. We like to share with you our stories and then leave you to think about it. This is to help you open your mind to greater learning, to higher possibilities.

The mind enjoys being stretched. When you do not work your mind, your mind becomes sad and dull. It will have no vision. You are created with the need to be creative and to be using your mind for the benefit for yourself and for the people you love close to you. Be inventive, use it well and the mind you have will be a treasure to you.

Do you realize your brain expands with every thought of positivity? Neurons enjoy being in the positive power of the thought. Memories become sharp. Understandings and connecting become more powerful. The brain shrinks with its pathways when there is suffering in the mind. It is then like a person who is walking in the desert without water. The lack of water is not good for the brain and as a result the brain becomes dry.

Your brain is created to expand and to think. When you understand how all things around you are energies of illusion and not as real as you think, your brain begins to understand this. It is designed to understand all these teachings.

You then become more connected within yourself, and begin to experience higher abilities, because you learn to switch your brain and mind to a higher accessible learning frequency.

Your world is as our world is also, surrounded in frequencies of light. You understand your radio waves. We listen to your radio waves. We tune into them because we are interested in your understanding of your life and we desire to help you progress. We tune into your TV channels and I must say, we enjoy the discovery channels but not the other presentations filled with hate and lack of love.

Why must the mind be filled with violence? Are you not learning that violence means the end of your generation and your world?

You must learn to choose wisely. Will you tune into the darkness; the side that must be discovered to learn about light? Or will you tune into light where you can learn about love?

Discoverers of dark you have been. You have been brave. You understand pain and hate. You understand unjust and hurt. However, it has been enough now has it not?

Learn to tune into love frequencies. Be in the joy of your life. When you are in the joy you are helping joy to become stronger on your plane. Your light is your lifeline and it is your key to living well in the future. Turn off your television screens when it is filled with violence. Learn to tune into yourselves.

How do you feel when you are seeing the sickening things of your society? Do you enjoy hearing about the murders and about the hurt on your planet?

You may argue with me. You may say you like to be 'in tune' with what is happening on your earth. Again, your pain becomes more of a reality by tuning into the pain.

Have you not learned throughout the ages? Do not give power to the ones who desire your pain on this plane. Refuse to live in the pain. Refuse to tune into the pain on your planet. Instead live in the joy in your own lives. Teach your children to grow good food on your land. Keep them busy in the light.

Greetings, I AM Halisarius, Pleadian Leader. I guide many Star Beings in the Love towards greater technology.

Your light body

Your light body,

is a body of flows and dimensions.

When you learn to reach,

into your body of light,

your higher understanding,

will be unlocked.

Then you will remember,

where to look.

You will find the keys,

you have been searching for.

The keys of:

Love,

Life,

Creation,

Power,

Existence,

because all is within you.

A Komo Ha Halima

Greetings, I AM Halisarius,
Pleiadian Chief Commander & Chief Leader,
Great Leader of the Galactic Federation of Light Society.

Part 9: Higher waves are awakening

We wish to greet you and welcome you to our frequency and our tune. When you read these pages, we gift you our love frequency as you learn to tune into your Pleiadian brothers and sisters in the light.

Over the last few lessons we have given you much information to absorb and to open the mind. Like you have learned, to learn is to expand the mind. We wish to give you further information to expand your mind and your neuron pathways within your brain.

We would like to help you understand more about you. You have abilities within you that you do not know you have. You are, as a race, spiritually opening with spiritual waveforms on your planet. More and more of you understand these gifts.

Many are afraid. Many are afraid of these experiences. Please hear us if you are afraid. If you are not afraid, we welcome you to these thoughts even more as we will transmit a third eye ray to you as you read these pages to help you open more to greater insight and understanding.

You are not closed beings of creation. You may believe it to be but the power of your belief becomes your reality. How does it reflect in your life? What stops your greater understanding?

It is the fear and misunderstandings you may have about these experiences of opening to higher spiritual waves. You may believe it to be wrong, again because you may have been taught differently. You may believe it to be frightening because you may believe that once you open to that 'other' side and 'other knowing,' it will become overwhelming for you.

Do you not understand that this is part of the patterning that has happened over many thousands of years? Do you not understand that your world desires to keep you away from your light?

You are created in high 'spiritual' waves. These energies are love energies. These energies of greater rays are powerful and when one reaches these energies within themselves, they are able to change their entire frequency and their world.

The power within you scares you more than anything. It is not the case of, 'In case I got it wrong,' or 'I will become overwhelmed.' The real fear is realization of the power within you.

You understand on your deeper levels that you hold an incredible strength and it frightens you. You have been led to believe that power within you is not the right belief to have.

Your society has been designed to keep you small and in your limitation. You have been kept in the dark with your powers. If you knew about yourself and how powerful you truly were, you would be able to change all of your society.

How would this change your society?

If you as a race awakened to the powers within you there would be no governments as you have now. Your governments would change because your core beliefs would change.

Your churches would have no followers. Much of the money systems would be gone as others would replace the way you would run your economic energies. Your hospitals would no longer be needed in the degree that they exist today.

Much of your society has been based on fear. Fear to keep you in the understanding that you are weak and that you hold no power within you.

Masses of people are opening to these spiritual waves now. They are part of the movement of the future, when you will discover the power energies within you and you will discover how to unify together, to bring change to your society.

You are becoming more telepathic and with the right training, you will understand how to bring yourselves together to use these gifts for the greater good and the higher will.

There will be more and more yearnings among you to learn how to access them, and you will question them. We ask you not to be afraid of them as they are gifts given to you from your creators. You are evolving into greater light and these are gifts for the great time of the Awakening.

Fear will keep you controlled by your leaders. Become free with the understanding of what is your truth.

Learn to access your higher powers and use them in the love. When you use them in the love, greater love will come back to you, as your life is your mirror reflecting back at you constantly.

I will greet you now. Greetings, I AM Halisarius, Pleiadian Chief Leader. I hold command. I help bring unity between the many Star Nations, leading them to greater evolution and peace.

When will you stop warring?

When will you stop warring?
When will you return to the great love?
When will you stop the pain within you?
When will you choose for love?
When will you stop your anger?
When will you stop your fear?
When will you learn,
to look within your heart?
There you will find,
your greater understanding,
your greater truth within,
your greater strength,
your greater wisdom,
your great eternal power,
your great eternal love,
for your Divinity.
When will you choose to look within,
your Sacred Eternal Heart?

A Komo Ha Halima

Greetings, I AM Halisarius,
Pleiadian Chief Commander & Chief Leader,
Great Leader of the Galactic Federation of Light Society.

Part 10: Celebrate your world

We wish to welcome you. We wish to greet you from our race and send love from us to you. How great it is to celebrate this time together as we are able to awaken you together.

It is time for your higher understanding, your closer connection and higher patterning of love to grow within you.

Love is greatly needed on your planet. Your planet is lacking the love in the hearts.

Energetically, the energies of your planet are of those in a higher dimension. Indeed you are in a cosmic party and you are becoming more and more in the greater light. You have light on your planet and light around you. Hence, you are awakening as a race because it is time for truth to come to you.

The hearts need greater love on your planet. How much you still anger over your past wars. You remind yourselves about the greater wars and how much the people suffered. Your fear for another catastrophe, in the same way, is great and you will attract it to yourselves if you do not change your ways of thinking.

You keep reminding yourselves and each other of the deaths. Should you not be celebrating life instead? You are alive and each day presents itself new opportunities for your further understanding to greatness and greater ways of being.

Instead, you dwell on your pain. Your children, who were not part of your war generations, have been taught well how the men suffered and died at the hands of their enemies.

The gassing gives your children nightmares. You are doing well keeping your fears and memories alive. It is like a fire that you keep feeding, to make sure it will not go out.

However friends, we teach you to expand your mind. How is your world doing with all this education? Is it teaching your young ones to love? Or is it feeding the energy of pain and hate?

We see everything as energy of illusions. You believe in your reality so it becomes true for you. What reality are you creating now? How much time are you spending on creating your destruction of your planet?

Each day, millions focus on war and killing. Many of your war soldiers, however, are forgotten about and they are suffering in silence, wanting to be recognized but largely forgotten.

We desire to help you to celebrate your life. Make days as celebration days when you unite together, when you learn to forgive each other and throw your weapons of destruction away, and when you do away with your evil thoughts of destruction, and of your fears. You will then learn the true celebration of life.

Be gone with them. Understand you are here to change your world. You are here to bring all things in the shadows to the light to be healed. Heal and then celebrate what you heal.

Celebrate your dreamers. Celebrate their themes. Celebrate their greatness. Encourage your young ones to follow their footsteps. Many of your young ones carry higher energies and higher understandings, and many of them are here to help you change your ways and your understandings.

Do not be proud of your wars any longer, for what is it changing now? Yes, it gave you freedom. Yes, it served a great purpose. Be thankful, but do not worship the energy of death any longer. Worship the love and the greatness instead. Then you will grow together in the love.

Greetings, I AM Halisarius, your friend and guide. On the higher star levels of love and light, I am also your commander and friend.

A Komo Ha Halima

Greetings, I AM Halisarius,
Pleiadian Chief Commander & Chief Leader,
Great Leader of the Galactic Federation of Light Society.

Part 11: You are the key to your future survival

We are here at this time to help you understand yourselves more. To understand yourself has been one of the greatest ventures you have had since the time of your creation.

You question the heavens. You question the earth. You question your leaders. You are in a great time of discovery and questioning. The more answers you have, the greater the questions become. The greater the discoveries become, the greater the understanding that you do not understand much at all, and there is still much discovery to be done.

You, in general, understand you are from the stars. You look at the stars, you pray to your heavenly beings for guidance, for deeper understanding and for deeper knowledge.

Yet, we say to you, do you not understand that what you are truly asking and seeking is to understand who you are and how great you are?

We ask you, if you knew that you did not need anyone else in the universe to help you to become free and to guide you to paradise, would that surprise you?

Like I have said in my pages previously, you believe you are limited. Many believe you came here to live as a sinner and then die as a sinner and then somehow you have become lost in the purpose of all.

We are helping you to understand that you are, 'The Great Discoverers' of your earth. You are, 'The Great Discoverers' to bring light back to your planet. Your planet needs light to become more in balance.

You are the key to your growth and to your existence on your planet. You are the key to your future survival and to your future happiness and evolution.

The key does not exist outside of yourselves; it exists within your hearts.

This may challenge your thinking once again. This is not generally taught to the people on your plane. You believe, in general, that you are limited and you require your governments to make the rules. You become sick and you need your doctors. You feel you have sinned and you need a priest to help you repent and be free.

These are beliefs entrenched within you over thousands and thousands of years. We are here to challenge those very beliefs. You will learn to look at your life differently.

We are now going to teach you about your history. You will want to read this and you will want to think about this.

How will this knowledge fit into your life? Will it change your views? Or perhaps will it keep you even more in pain?

We will leave that decision up to you dear friends.

Nothing is what it seems. Nothing in your existence or your history is what it seems. Indeed, you think you see something and you believe it to be and it becomes your reality.

Greetings, I AM Halisarius, Pleiadian Leader. I am a Great Leader of the Galactic Federations of Light. There are many Federations. All for the purpose to help the universes evolve to love and light and Divine Purpose.

A Komo Ha Halima

Greetings, I AM Halisarius,
Pleiadian Chief Commander & Chief Leader,
Great Leader of the Galactic Federation of Light Society.

Part 12: Light and dark live together

We desire to help you understand your journey better. Your journey to discover more about your life and understand how you fit into the grand scheme of things.

You came here to be the discoverers of light.

Please understand friends, that the universe is infinite. It keeps expanding and it is alive with greatness and with intelligence. There are many beings outside of your plane. Many of them are discovers of light, like you are, and many of them do not wish to be with light.

This is because no one is forced to believe in one or the other. Light and dark reside together. There cannot be light, unless dark lives with light. How can light see truth and greatness unless dark exposes what is not truly light?

You live in a realm of light and dark. Light is upon your earth. You are discovering much about working with light and many of you are awakening to the love on your planet.

However, how can you discover true light and the importance of light, when dark stays undiscovered?

You must discover darkness and pain before light becomes stronger.

As it has been on your planet, it has also been on many other planets. There are those of us, (star beings) who dwell in full light. However, we have grown towards full light with our evolution and our lessons of growth. Many others have also done their time with expansion into full light.

All star beings are on a different path of evolution.

Some are travelers and time jumpers. They like to discover how to move ahead with their scientific discoveries. Others are scientists in different fields. There are those who create life on planets and create new species. There are those who desire to work with frequencies and vibrations of sound and light to create change.

There are those of defiance, who are not friendly and have battled with beings of light who have desired peace and love.

Great battles in the universes have happened in history. We have written these down in our history books to learn from. Not to celebrate, but to learn from in order for them not to ever happen again.

Earth was created for a definite purpose. Earth was not placed in the universe for a reason that was small.

Greetings, I AM Halisarius, Pleiadian Teacher and Leader. You remember me well when you begin to work with my energies. I am calling all who desire to return to the Great Star Levels of love and peace.

Each one on your planet is very important to Divine

Each one on your planet,

is very important to Divine.

All upon your plane,

carry a vibration,

a tune,

so unique in itself.

This is your tune given to you,

by your greater self,

as your greater self,

in the greater love dimensions,

is praying you will awaken.

When you awaken,

you will begin to see,

a whole new perspective of life.

you will begin,

to become a new creation.

A new journey will then begin.

A Komo Ha Halima

Greetings, I AM Halisarius,
Pleiadian Chief Commander & Chief Leader,
Great Leader of the Galactic Federation of Light Society.

Part 13: Are you ready to expand your mind?

We wish to greet you on this wonderful journey of your light journey. We like to help you understand greater aspects of your life, so that you gain the understanding for all of life.

I would like to continue from our last discussion about your planet.

Your planet is significant. Your planet is filled with nourishment and life. It is the planet of life. Though it may be a small planet compared to many other planetary bodies, it is filled with treasures.

Many of these treasures of your ancient history are still to be discovered. It has not been the time to discover all your treasures just yet, because your mind still needs to be opened for greater discoveries to be found.

For instance, many believe that you came from prehistoric beings. So you will find your 'evidence' as it were, to fit your theories. Your understanding then becomes more 'solid' with your findings and indeed, many people around your world grasp these theories as they feel themselves satisfied with the answers.

Can you not see when you desire to find your evidence you will find it? However, do these findings prove your history? Or do they prove your theories?

After all, we Pleiadians of Light are endeavoring to teach you, you are living in an illusion created together with your consciousness. We are also helping you discover your past and your history.

There are many people that do not believe in evolution as many scientists believe it to be, and thus their questions become even greater.

You are a young race compared to many other planetary beings and yet much older than many of you believe you to be.

You are created with a purpose to find greater ways of exploring yourselves. You are in a theatre play. Many star beings are watching your theatre as the energies play themselves out on your planet.

You may not see it that way. You may ask, 'Theatre play? If so, in what theatre play are we involved in?'

Be patient my friends, as you will find out many of these answers within these pages. We desire to help you expand your mind as then you will remember many of the events that played out in your history.

Please do not jump the pages of this book to try and find the answers quickly, because then we cannot give you our rays of transmissions as you are reading, to help to enlighten you on your history and your greater purpose.

All of life is a game. It is not as real as you believe it to be. All of life, everything you see with your eyes, you are seeing in your eye's mind. You think you see it with your physical eyes, but what you are seeing is energy and your mind is translating it into what you believe it to be.

This, in itself, may be a great mystery to you, but if you are open to these ideas and riddles, you will be able to work out many new inventions on your planet.

Consider it friends and ask these energies to reveal new ways of living to you. You will be surprised with their response.

You are highly intelligent. You are more intelligent than you realize at this moment. We know you will access higher gifts on your journey in the near future; only when you begin to realize what your reality is all about.

Your belief of seeing everything as real and solid stops much of your expansion and evolution. You believe your solidness and you believe you cannot change it. This gives you fear because you believe you cannot do much about your world. You believe life has given it to you. However, this is far from truth.

If you could understand, you would revolutionize all things on your planet.

We will discuss this further in this book. How much we are giving you to think about. How much have you expanded in your ideas?

Have you considered how wonderful your life could be if you could understand your true purpose on your plane? For then your life would make much more sense to you.

I will return with another lesson of your life. Greetings, I AM Halisarius, your Guide and Teacher.

A Komo Ha Halima

Greetings, I AM Halisarius,
Pleiadian Chief Commander & Chief Leader,
Great Leader of the Galactic Federation of Light Society.

Part 14: You are involved in the game of life

Could it really be that we, Pleiadians, exist? Could it be that other beings are watching you and are truly living in a different world of existence?

Many people on your earth are accepting other beings to be alive, for you are searching and are looking for the great evidence.

Yes, we are living on another dimension on another planetary system. We have several planets. We are often called the Seven Sisters by you and we celebrate each other.

Here we are teaching about you, your history and how you came to be here. The topic is vast. How can you explain eternity?

I mentioned earlier in these pages within this book, how there are in existence beings that are not living in light and those of us who live in light.

There are many planetary beings, as you will have gathered by now, who are watching you and watching how your game will unfold. Much is at stake for each of us as star beings and also for you.

Some planetary beings do not want you to be enlightened and most of us do.

We desire you to understand these teachings and to implement them in your life so you become the greatest you can possibly be, so that you evolve in light so that we reunite together as brothers and sisters of the Great Family of Light.

Some beings desire fear and pain on your planet. They desire this because they do not want light on your planet. Light on your planet would go against their wishes. They desire to control the universal planetary beings.

Indeed, the game is large and you are a speck in the ocean of vastness of the universal bodies of existence.

This paragraph I have just transmitted through my channel, I would like you to read and re-read, to help you understand the significance of the game you are involved in.

Could it be that there are great wars still happening in the great universal energies of planetary existences?

Could it be that we are fighting for our freedom and this is why it is important to help you understand the significance of your being here today?

Could it be that we desire to join you in our fight also to gain the greatness and unification back in the universe so that peace will exist forever?

A Komo Ha Halima, Greetings, I AM Halisarius, your Friend and Teacher in these spaces and in the higher spaces of love.

Your beautiful earth

Your beautiful earth,

is rich with treasures.

Your earth is a code within itself,

waiting to reveal,

its ancient history,

its sacred secrets,

its truth,

to enrich you,

to bless you,

to awaken the Great Love within you,

within your Golden Heart,

which is great love,

on the greater dimensions.

Grow into the love of your Great Being.

Become love.

A Komo Ha Halima

Greetings, I AM Halisarius,
Pleiadian Chief Commander & Chief Leader,
Great Leader of the Galactic Federation of Light Society.

Part 15: We are your caretakers of your planet

Greetings, I have returned. How wonderful it is that I can speak to you through these pages. I AM Halisarius and I care greatly for the planets of our systems. We are part of the Galactic Federation and we take active part in creating great positive changes between us, the Pleiadians, and other beings.

We love our brothers and sisters in the light and we work together with our Teacher Guides in Spirit of the Pleiades and our Archangels in light.

We are highly intelligent and we operate our computers differently than you. You will also advance to the levels we are at in your future. We use our minds to operate them and we create our technology with them and they are perfectly accurate. We are able to adjust them to our liking and we expand with our knowledge every day.

We have many scientists and work hard keeping your atmosphere clean. Do you realize many poisons and radioactivity comes from your earth to the stars? This could be incredibly damaging as all creation is ecologically sensitive. As you are killing your planet with these poisons so you are also creating damage on other planets.

Part of our job is to keep the atmosphere around you clear of poison. We are your caretakers as it were because we care very much for the planet you are on and the planets around you.

You do not understand yet how much damage you are creating on your planet each day.

A long, long time ago, your planet thrived with life. Your animals, your treasures, your minerals thrived. It was rich and it was good. It was loved by star beings.

Many star beings came to your planet and planted their DNA blueprint within many species and created many plants and animals on your earth. They were pleased to do this to help you remember your brothers and sisters in the light.

They planted their footprints, literally and symbolically upon your earth, to help you have a home to be happy in.

They were happy to be part of the play that would happen on your planet.

Your planet is unique. Your oceans, all those times ago, were thriving with life from other universes, to help you evolve and live great lives.

The human was created. Where did you come from? How did you come into your existence? Did you come from apes, or perhaps some other prehistoric being?

You will discover this knowledge in the following stories. As you do, we would like to help you remember your past and history.

You all have your history within you. We are here to help you remember.

Your past has many surprises, although it may not seem as mysterious once we have opened you to the energies of this knowledge as you will resonate with it. Or will you choose to fight it?

Greetings, I AM Halisarius, Pleiadian Chief Commander. I am an ancient being of great love with much wisdom to share for your growth.

A Komo Ha Halima

Greetings, I AM Halisarius,

Pleiadian Chief Commander & Chief Leader,

Great Leader of the Galactic Federation of Light Society.

Part 16: Learning to live in the present rather than the past

How great it is to have you with us once again. You thirst for knowledge. You thirst for understanding. You thirst for knowledge of your ancestors and knowledge of the stars.

I wish to bring your attention to the present once again. Why are we going back and forth? We are going back and forth because the present has much to do with your history.

Your history is where it all began. Your present is where the game is played. Your present is always more important than your past. The past has been. Your present is here.

We ask you to understand you more. Have you considered your desires within you? What are they? How will they be awakened with all this knowledge? Will you change? Will you see life differently? Will your pain and fear go with greater knowledge? How will that change you?

The fear and anger have kept many in a prison of life. You cannot receive the joy of your life with pain and anger in your life. You cannot see the greatness of your life if you live in fear. Your society has been held down by fear.

Now, you are living in a time where you are able to speak out more freely and discover more. You are living in a time where you are able to understand more about who it is that you are and your freedom is becoming greater.

However, for many of you, the memories of the past are still present and hold you back.

Your memories of being tortured and feelings as if others will not accept you for who you are, are still present. Many of your people find it hard to stand up and tell others their beliefs.

Greetings I AM Halisarius, Pleiadian Leader. I bring many blessings from the Star Races of love to you.

A Komo Ha Halima

Greetings, I AM Halisarius,
Pleiadian Chief Commander & Chief Leader,
Great Leader of the Galactic Federation of Light Society.

Part 17: Your secret you hold within is powerful

I am here to help you understand more about yourselves. You are in a time of incredible history where you begin to join the pieces together, but with this information also, you will be opening your mind up to many greater understandings.

We wish to help you with understanding the power within you. First we will introduce who you are and then we will continue with the teachings that we have to share with you.

We have stories to tell you about yourselves. However, if these pages would show them directly to you, many would shut their minds to the greater information. Why? This is because you have been trained to mistrust. You have been trained not to allow too much information into your mind that could open your mind. You like to have certain things put into your mind and not much beyond it. You do not even realize the extent of your programming.

This is largely because of the fear that has been placed within your memories. Your cellular system holds the memories and emotions of all your lifetimes. Your DNA holds the coding of who you really are. You are a treasure and a library filled with information.

If you understood the reality of what you were and who you are you would revolutionize your world.

Many beings on the outer fringes of your universe, who have found you and who are studying you and observing you in this large game you are involved in, have already discovered why mankind is powerful. Many envy you and desire what you have. Many fear it also, because if you unlocked yourselves, you could travel to their planets and bring your gift of love to them and bring healing, even for those who resent light. This could change all energies of the universal systems and create a bigger play.

However, because of your fear and your greed, you cannot find the secret until you learn to understand greater ways and understand how to let go of your anger.

Anger has shut your greater abilities down. Anger has caused much disharmony on your planet in greater ways than you understand. You may think you are far away from troubled spots, or you may think you live in a different age than your large world wars, but the energies are present everywhere.

These energies of fear and of anger are infectious and until you learn to walk freely with the energies of love, you will not be cleared from them and you cannot change your plane.

You hold such a history within your cellular system and this history does not stop at your present life right now. It comes from all your generations, your grandparents and so on, your past lives, your world views, your traditions and cultures, your religions.

How can you not be confused? You must understand this in order to understand and unravel the secrets within you. You are complicated beings. You also hold a great secret within you. If you are able to unfold it, it will change who you are and it could change the very surface of the earth and make it more inviting for us as your Star Brothers and Sisters to rejoin you as old friends.

Greetings, I AM Halisarius, Pleiadian Leader. I am here to bring you the love from the greater love bodies of Universal Love.

A Komo Ha Halima

Greetings, I AM Halisarius,
Pleiadian Chief Commander & Chief Leader,
Great Leader of the Galactic Federation of Light Society.

Part 18: The beauty of who you are

I wish to return now with another teaching. We like to teach you as we have many stories to tell you. We are your record keepers because you are part of a great play in your history and in our greater universal system.

In the pages of this book you will find secrets, secrets that you must note down in order to find the great clues of who you are.

As you are reading these words, you are also receiving Pleiadian Rays to help you understand the information. Within these words are codes to help you unravel the person you are and touch you in ways to help you expand your mind and to find truth of your universe.

Many are awakening to this information. Many are still wondering and many others are afraid.

Fear has been placed within your cellular memory a long, long time ago. You were not like you are now hundreds of thousands of years ago.

I would like to introduce you to the way you used to be. This is a story and we are good storytellers. With stories, we educate our young ones on our planets and we find their learning is greater than if we tell them facts.

The mind likes stories, it likes to imagine and it likes to visualize.

Do you realize that your brain is created this way to visualize and imagine? Do you know that if you tap into those abilities, you become happier and freer within yourself?

Your society is based on shutting that side down, though masses are awakening to this. You are speaking out more freely now. You think and create more freely now.

In your darker days, mankind was not permitted to go to the creative mind. You used to say to each other, 'Heavens forbid.' If only you knew how correct this statement was.

Using the creative mind is a portal to everything that is outside of your reality and into the energies of true reality.

Time does not have a beginning or an ending and is largely created by the mind when it believes it to be true.

Have you not noticed that when you create and sit silently that time seems to 'fly by?' You do not remember where the time has gone? This is because at these times you escape your reality of your life by going into another 'zone' as it were, leaving your logical reality of thought.

This is what you are designed to do. When you are in these spaces, you create, you extract, you design and you think. In these spaces you are happy, you invent and you connect. When you are studying and only use the part of the brain that uses logic, without accessing the creative side, you are not expanding the mind as you would like it to. You are not designed that way.

You were created with a brain to continuously expand in greater understanding. Your brain, in many ways, mirrors your universe. There are many neurons connecting to each other, like the planetary systems connecting to each other. Nothing is separate from one another. The database chambers stored in your brain are like the databases stored in the universes. Each universe has a story to tell and when we connect the information it would fill up much more than all the libraries on your planet.

Your brain is designed to expand and to keep living for thousands of years. You have an incredible gift. The universe also keeps expanding as it is infinite with information and understanding.

As you see from this simple illustration, you hold the keys to your vast universe. You are able to tap into this information when you tap into your greatness within your mind. When you understand the power you hold in the grand scheme of things, you will have the power to stop all your disease on your planet and create abundance.

Greetings, I AM Halisarius, Pleiadian Leader and Chief Advisor of the Galactic Federation of Light Society. I am here to guide you upwards to who you truly are.

A Komo Ha Halima

Greetings, I AM Halisarius,
Pleiadian Chief Commander & Chief Leader,
Great Leader of the Galactic Federation of Light Society.

Part 19: Your earth; a precious gift from your Star Brothers and Sisters

Your planet is a jewel and is magnificent. The waters she holds gives life to all. The earth is perfectly balanced and she has many treasures she has not revealed to you yet. She has the ability to give you everything you require and beyond to heal.

Yet, she is hurting. The very secrets she would like to share with you she cannot as yet, because you will destroy it. You will create money with her treasures, instead of using it to heal the people.

Many of her gifts have not been used for healing but for trade. Too often she has been used and abused.

Please make no mistake dear ones, she knows and understands your thoughts and intentions. She hurts and we hear her screams asking us to help her, to somehow share with you how important she is and how she is dying.

To her, you are like the vultures that came to your planet who took your pride and love and great dignity.

You, as a whole, have also done this to your earth. Her pride has gone, her love for herself has greatly been lost and she has lost her dignity.

We, and many others of your star brothers and sisters, still to this day celebrate the cycles of your earth. You used to celebrate them also. Many still do on your planet. Your earth loves being celebrated. She loves to be reminded of the greater times of who she truly is.

You wonder why there are many storms and many acts of violence from her. Can you not see dear ones that she is reacting to your pain and she is reflecting your consciousness as a whole? The anger you hold and lash out towards each other in fear and war, she is also feeling and you will sense her pain with turbulence and great shaking.

Learn to love yourselves and forgive each other. Then, she will also heal and settle down.

You say your planet is overpopulated and yet there is room for many millions more. However, the way your planet has been destroyed and poisoned, you have stopped your own growth. Your earth cannot feed that many people and provide your nurturing.

Yet, it was given to you with the gift of life, the gift of learning to become more at peace and love. Do you see how beautiful your earth is? It is far more beautiful on the greater level than many of the planets within the greater space of the universe.

Again, your planet was created with a particular reason. The reason was to share the beauty of all of life and what life can be like. It was given to you to remember the greatest gifts within you that would benefit, not only you on the earth, but also in the grander scheme of things.

This earth is so special that thousands upon thousands of species from other planets came to your earth to plant their footprints on your planet.

You tend to wonder, how come we do not notice you? Why do you feel all alone in the existence of the grand universe?

Yet, how does it feel for you to know that we, as well as many others are watching you every day? Many of your star brothers and sisters wonder if they did enough for you in your history to awaken you. Will you remember?

You are beautiful

You are beautiful,

an extraordinary creation,

more magnificent than you know,

powerful,

gifted with gifts you cannot comprehend.

Yet these gifts,

are very hidden,

waiting to be discovered by you.

You hold the keys,

to your greater evolution,

to ascend upwards to join,

The Great Family of Light.

You are a creation,

of powerful beings of love.

You have the gifts,

of your Powerful Grand Creators.

But, will you awaken to them collectively?

A Komo Ha Halima

Greetings, I AM Halisarius,
Pleiadian Chief Commander & Chief Leader,
Great Leader of the Galactic Federation of Light Society.

Part 20: The reason why you came to earth

We come to you now because you are in a time of Great Awakening. It is a time where you will understand more about you.

Your earth is filled with treasures and with knowledge of your ancestors and where you come from. Many of these treasures have been found. Much evidence has been found. Not everything is revealed to you at this time as your whole society would face change because of the knowledge if it were to be revealed. You have not found it yet because you are not ready yet. If you found these ancient treasures, much fear would come upon your plane. The panic would be great.

People on your plane have been controlled for a long time. You may say you may not feel controlled now. 'Gone are those days,' you may say.

We say differently. You are very much controlled. You are controlled in the ways you dress, speak, learn, work and make love. You are not free at all.

Perhaps you may not see it in these ways but you are far from free. How can you feel free when you carry fear within you? You carry it with you wherever you go. The fear of your planet not supporting your life and your children, the fear of you losing your jobs or the way your health may deteriorate, the fear of your insecure future.

Fear becomes your reality and hence your belief systems within the fear become stronger, because you are creating your fears together.

We say you are very much controlled. Being controlled by fear and power is the way the leaders of your world have kept you in the dark from who you truly are.

You are not only physical, though you have been led to believe you are. You have many dimensions of life. You are multidimensional. You hold gifts within you, you do not understand, like we have said many times before throughout these pages.

Are you willing to discover you and who you are? Or are you willing to stay stuck in your fear and your pain?

The choosing is up to the individual. Again, we cannot make that choice for you. You can only make the choices for yourselves. You can only gain the understanding for yourselves.

You are far from what you appear to be. You create your everyday reality. You look in the mirror and you see a face that is yours. Why do you see the same face? Because you have trained your mind well to believe it is your face.

Your mind is incredibly powerful. Because it is incredibly powerful it has created your reality. If you choose to discover the laws outside of your reality, you may well become surprised. You would work against your fearful belief systems and come to the realization that everything we say is correct.

Like we have said before in these pages, your mind is incredibly powerful.

Your mind likes to stay safe. This is because of what has been instructed to you over many tens of thousands of years, when everything changed within you.

You were no longer free to travel with your star brothers and sisters to discover the stars and discover other realities of being. You were now locked into a reality of fear, control and pain.

We are guiding you to become free from this reality of pain you believe to be real to help you understand truth. However, you can only make that choice.

What choice do you have? You have several. You can learn about the information that has been sent to you, from the Pleiadian Realms of Light Beings. We are trying to guide you and help you through this maze of entanglement created by people who desire to rule you. We are trying to guide you and free you from beings who are feeding from your fear to become more powerful. However, you always have the choice to refuse to go to these ideas and keep suffering in your pain.

Many of you will listen to these ideas because these ideas are not new. Hence, you are able to grow upon them and learn more. We have given you keys all along during these times to help you to grow and understand who you are and where you are from. You are now ready to learn more about yourselves and to find greater keys to your higher existence.

There are those who do not want you to find out who you are. They have gone to great lengths to keep you in limitation and in your weakness. They have done well in sucking your powers towards them so that you cannot use them.

When you understand the truth of what has been going on for many, many tens of thousands of years you will learn to claim your truth back to use it to free your lives from enslavement.

You are enslaved. You have grown up in your society and lived many incarnations on this earth. You do not remember what it is like to be free and to live in the joy of all that is.

Why did you come here? Why did you come here to discover more about life? What is the soul family of light doing on your earth? Is it to understand technology? Is it to understand the human body more? Is it to save planet earth? Is it to contact outer (from your perspective) space beings?

If we wanted to contact you, and I speak for many of the races from the many planetary systems of life existence, we would have contacted you a long time ago. We know you are there. Our technology is far more advanced that you realize. We hear you via your waves. We see you via your waves. We can tune into your plans and into your thoughts.

Primarily, you are here to rediscover the powers within you that frighten the very people who are your leaders.

You are here to rediscover the essential ingredient within you that many other beings envy.

What is this connection within you?

It is the love connection.

Love you may say? 'I find it hard to find love,' you may reason.

You understand the sensation, the energy of love. Love has been deadened in the hearts of many. Many are confused with love. They do not understand what it is.

Many understand it be to sexually attracted to another. However, that phase quickly disappears when one has not found true love for each other.

You have love for much. Love for your children and love for your lives and partners.

We encourage you to investigate more about your love, for your love is your key to your powers. It is the key to understanding your higher gifts and your multidimensional selves. It is the key to finding your freedom from all pain and fear placed within you.

I will leave you with this to absorb and register within you. You will feel truth within these pages.

Love is a frequency

Love is a frequency,

within your Sacred Secret Heart.

You have forgotten how to reach it,

how to unlock the sacred love within you,

until now,

when the doors are opening,

for your greater love.

These are the sacred times,

of your Grand Sacred Heart Opening.

Learn to feel within the frequency,

within your Sacred Golden Heart.

Learn to flow with your great love,

within these golden gates,

hidden deep within you.

A Komo Ha Halima

Greetings, I AM Halisarius,
Pleiadian Chief Commander & Chief Leader,
Great Leader of the Galactic Federation of Light Society.

Part 21: Great Light is here

In the last pages, we have already given you much to chew on. How much are you absorbing? How much do you understand?

We understand your programming and as you are reading these messages we desire to help your cells remember who you truly are so that you will make the changes in your lives to overcome the fear of your society.

Your life is abundant with opportunities to grow every day. Your mind is filled with the answers for your life. Your mind is developed in such a way to keep expanding.

Your emotions hold a great key to your expansion. Within the emotion there is a pattern of growth and of bondage. The pain and the sadness keep you in bondage and each time you are in these emotions, your cells help you to remember your pain well.

When you are in the joy, your cells also help you to remember those memories.

Can you understand the importance of working together with your cellular memories? Can you understand how important it is to focus on the parts within you that hold your great keys to your health and positive outlook and outcome?

You are programmed to believe you become old and so you do. You are programmed to believe that you need your governments and so you feel comfortable with the ideas of having to give them your power, for if you do not you are threatened by your system and by the people around you. You have done well in following the wishes of your leaders.

Two thousand years ago your history changed as light came upon the earth and awakened much upon your planet.

A man you call Jesus came to your plane. He showed people how to become free within them.

Many of the stories about Jesus have been exaggerated for the purpose of keeping you in fear and bondage with fear and control. Many of the stories are not true and much has been eliminated. You are led to believe he was the savior, and yet, he never said it. He was simply there to show light as a way shower. Much of that light stayed in your existence until now when it is time for light to flourish on your plane once again.

There have been many way showers in your history who have brought the light. This man Jesus showed the people in those days how to live in the light and how to be strong. Many resisters did not like the way he taught. He gave the freedom and power back to the people. The leaders took him away, out of the scene.

In those days, the leaders did not like to be argued with. Jesus was a peaceful man. He used power with his speech. He was a channel of love, of the Greatest Archangels in the light and a channel of the Great Divine One. He showed the way of freedom to the people.

That light he brought remained on the earth. At times it seemed as if they, the dark, had won once again by taking light away from the people.

However, light remained and it was strong enough to survive until the time of the Great Awakening. The Great Awakening was the time the great prophets spoke about many thousands of years ago; the 'Restoration of Light and Consciousness.'

What time are you in now friends? You are in the time of the Great Light. You are now in the time of light that many spoke about many thousands of years ago. Prophecies have been written and many prophecies have been destroyed in fear you would find the light and unravel your strength and your power.

If you knew the fear your leaders have of you finding out the strength within you, you would be surprised and amazed, for they do everything to keep you in limitation.

I will return with another awakening lesson.

Greetings, I AM Halisarius, Pleiadian Chief Leader. We as Pleiadians pray you will awaken to the sacred gifts within you.

A Komo Ha Halima

Greetings, I AM Halisarius,

Pleiadian Chief Commander & Chief Leader,

Great Leader of the Galactic Federation of Light Society.

Part 22: Learn to be in the power of joy

At this time we would like to help you understand your joy. How important it is to be joyful on your planet.

To have joy is a difficult task for many people on your plane. How many of you smile at just being and having your life? How many are appreciative of every day?

Your society has created joy to be a challenge. Your focus is on the challenges instead of the joy. We are talking in general terms.

What has this created on your planet? More sorrow, more wars, more crime, more earthquakes, more flooding, more food shortages, more insecurity and more disease.

Are you surprised to hear us say this? Yet, as we have discussed in these pages previously, your reality is created with your mind and all your thoughts become your mirror.

How often do you only meditate on the joy and the greatness of your life? Or how much time do you spend investigating your pain and talking to each other about your pain?

It is these talks and emotions and heavy thought forms that create your pain largely on your plane.

If you understand this teaching, please work towards creating joy on your plane in your life every day. Be happy and be in the joy, for then your world will carry greater joy.

You were not created to have pain. This belief that you must be in the pain is far from truth. Yes, we teach you why you have discovered the pain of the dark. How can light be understood without understanding dark first? This is why you discovered dark with light, so that you can triumph and win from darkness and transform it into light.

Yet, your original purpose was not to be in fear and pain, but to be in the joy. Joy is where the great powers are. They are hidden like gems within your hearts. Can you see them coming to life? Can you sense them within your hearts? How wonderful it is when you can, our friends. We, as your Pleiadian brothers and sisters, desire to walk with you and teach you the great benefits of joy.

Some of you cannot comprehend joy; how great these energies are. You will say, 'How can someone be in joy constantly?'

Yet, we say you can. You can learn to become that way.

You live in a higher dimension of frequencies when you live in joy. The greater you begin to experience your game within light plays, the less you will want to join the heavier energies of play.

I will return with another lesson. Greetings, I AM Halisarius. Please awaken to who you are. When you join the greater spaces you become part of the Greater Family of Light.

Together you create your world

Together you create your world,

your beauty,

your growth,

your love,

your fear,

your disease,

your wars and pain.

Learn to understand the power within you.

Return to your heart.

Unlock the love within you.

Learn to create collectively,

a world filled with love,

with harmony,

with peace,

with growth,

with warmth,

so that all creation upon the earth,

is greatly blessed by Divine Love.

A Komo Ha Halima

Greetings, I AM Halisarius,

Pleiadian Chief Commander & Chief Leader,

Great Leader of the Galactic Federation of Light Society.

Part 23: Awaken creators, awaken to who you are

How wonderful it is that we are able to share with you our thoughts from the Pleiadian records of history, of your history. Your history is crucial to the game in the universe, to the theatre of play.

You are involved in an experimental game that will win, we are sure. We are certain that you will wake up to your light within you, as masses will yearn for this understanding.

How else will you change your ways? How else will you learn to live in greater and higher ways of love? You are created to search for yourselves within yourselves and how you are yourselves. You are created to yearn to understand your 'gods' because you believe they have higher powers than you have.

We say to you, do you truly believe this to be so? Perhaps they have this power because they understood the power of creation, whereas you do not just yet. However, when you awaken to who you are and how multidimensional you are and the creative force within you, is it then not possible that you could also create new species of life?

Here we would like to expand the mind once again. With our stories and our ways of teachings, there are good reasons behind us teaching in these ways. Because each thought opens you up to a higher thought within your mind. We hope to speak to your mind in such a way that you begin to understand and remember your history and who you truly are.

You speak of your 'God' as a holy creator, one with an immense power. However, what if your reasoning is nothing else but a belief that has been placed within you to make you believe it to be so, to make you fearful of authority and of not doing as you are told?

You are very proficient at following when you are in fear of not understanding your truth. You will not feel within what truth is and what is not because of fear, which has been implanted within you many, many tens of thousands of years ago and it still exists within your cellular memory. That memory is more alive than ever within your cells.

Your memories are just like those of yesterday within your cells. You hear of an event that could possibly happen in your solar system and on your earth. You prepare for it well, in case it causes a catastrophe. Your fear is immense.

Your fear is based on nothing but because you fear it so much, your energy bodies act out the very fears within you. You are your own commanders and your own creators and you have not woken up to that just yet.

Hence, we are here to help you wake up.

What if all this was not just a story, but was truly happening around you? What if your stories of your powerful God were not true? How would that affect you? How would it affect your thinking if you knew that fear was placed within your cellular memory to control you and to make you limited in everything you knew to be?

What if it was so, that everything you feared you created as a society together? How would this open your mind?

How will this knowledge change your ways of doing your everyday duties? Will it change? Will you begin to change your thoughts? Will you begin to see how important it is to change the ways you think and fear and how important it is to be more in the love?

As you see from these pages our friends, change is needed on your plane. Your plane is in the midst of these changes that we are assisting you with.   We are able to share with you more of who you truly are.

Greetings, I AM Halisarius, Pleiadian Chief and Commander. We are waiting for the greater numbers to desire love and light.

Your inheritance of your perfect DNA

Your inheritance,

of your perfect DNA,

was perfect,

flawless,

powerful,

beautiful,

because you did not know,

the ways of fear,

the ways of pain,

the ways of anger.

You lived in dimensions of Pure Love.

In those dimensions you grew,

into your greatness.

Return to the great love.

Return to the greatness.

You will then find the love dimensions,

you are looking for.

A Komo Ha Halima

Greetings, I AM Halisarius,

Pleiadian Chief Commander & Chief Leader,

Great Leader of the Galactic Federation of Light Society.

Part 24: A peek into your history

As you have read these pages, you are able to see yourselves more in a mirror. How will you view your society after opening your mind? Are you experiencing new thoughts and ideas? Are you considering how you can create change in your life? Or do you not believe these stories?

If you do not believe these stories we have shared thus far, please ask yourself this question: 'What are you afraid of? How is it affecting the way you have seen your life to be?'

All life, as we have shared with you before, is an illusion. An ocean filled with illusions. You are able to create your reality based on your beliefs you have created together.

Have you considered how important you are together? If one person can create a change within his or her life with the thought, imagine how powerful it is when groups come together with the thought.'

This is what we also discovered, like we have shared with you in these pages previously. We discovered we created together. We could create our life together. We discovered how to access our dimensional higher bodies and create stronger bodies.

Yes, our bodies are built differently than yours, although the same in many ways. We live in a higher dimension, so we are not physical as you are, though we can create a physical body if we desire to.

This may surprise you. Yes, we are also multidimensional like you are. You are also able to access this gift of your greater dimensions. Many in the ancient times could do this.

Let me take you back some time. Allow me to share with you how people lived in the ancient times.

This was a long time ago. We are story tellers and we enjoy our stories. Please open your imagination.

At that time earth was different. It was luscious and green. The air was not polluted. The earth was perfect. No wars and no crimes. Perfection was present on your planet. No one died needlessly until it was time to return 'home.' You could choose your own time to go 'home.' You had time to say goodbye to your friends and family.

You would choose your time when you had discovered enough of your planet. This could be a few hundred years after your birth, or a few thousand years after your birth.

There was no fear. No one understood war or earthquakes. Famine was not something known to your planet. Earth was in abundance and love was abundant.

Everyone alive had a gift to share with another and because the love for each other was great, that gift was shared with everyone else. Some had the great gift of understanding the mind, how to use it to create. Others understood how to disappear and appear. As you can imagine, the greatest joys and discoveries were made.

People talked to the earth. They understood the earth and her frequencies. They would bring the frequencies down from the star planetary systems into the earth, so the earth could thrive.

Do you want to know how your flowers came about? Yes, you may say from a seed? But did the flower come first? Or the seed? How was it placed on your earth?

We will tell you largely with the imagination. You were able to come together with one thought. You thought about a flower and you thought about a gift that flower could give from the universe and there it was.

Each flower on your planet has a frequency of light from star beings of love. Have you considered this? Have you considered how your flowers know your thoughts? Have you considered your flowers are teaching you how to love more?

Everything has been given to you to awaken you to your greater powers.

Again, we will leave you with this thought.

Greetings, I AM Halisarius, Pleiadian Teacher. I help all Pleiadians to evolve to greater love.

A Komo Ha Halima

Greetings, I AM Halisarius,
Pleiadian Chief Commander & Chief Leader,
Great Leader of the Galactic Federation of Light Society.

Part 25: We are your Guardians

We wish to come in peace and as friends, to help you understand yourselves more, to awaken you to your powers within, to who you are and to assist you in your growth.

How long we have longed for this time of reunion. It has been long. It has been a time of discovery for you.

Many thousands of years ago, we were your regular visitors from the stars. We sat with you and taught you many ways of the stars, to help you advance with your technology.

You learned quickly. You learned our gifts and we gave you all we could at that time, knowing we could not give you everything we knew because you needed to evolve at your own speed.

There were those who took advantage of our precious gifts and turned our gifts into battles of war. We were greatly hurt by those people who took our gifts of love from you. We gave them to you to help you advance with your technology and with your ways of life. Our gifts to you were taken to destroy yourselves and others.

How much we mourned you. How much we loved you. We could not help you any further until thousands of years later, slowly guiding you back to who you truly were.

We were not upset or angry, however we were sad. We felt for you. We knew we could no longer help you. Your civilization drew back. Your technology fell back greatly. Your understanding today is still not as great as back then in many ways but you cannot advance to that level yet, until you have lost the greed and the anger, for with the knowledge that we can share with you, you would destroy your planet and yourselves because of your greed and anger.

Destroying your planet is far from what we desire, as well as the desire of many other planetary beings, including the Great Universal Light. We work together with your Angels who are also guiding you to your light.

There is much to lose in the grand scheme of play should your planet be destroyed. We make sure you will not destroy your planet.

Many times, we have interrupted your destruction plans. If you knew how many times you would have destroyed your planet over and over, many people on your plane would be shocked.

However, we are taking care of you, not because of the human race especially, but mainly because of the Divine Purpose of all things.

You are discovering slowly your greater purpose of existence through these pages. Are you feeling the changes within you yet? Are you opening your mind yet?

We like to open your mind. As you are reading these lessons that are yours at this special time, we are transmitting to you rays from our Realms of the Pleiadian Light Beings to you.

We are strong with our thought. We understand the grand scheme and we know the importance of our play as well.

When we reveal it to you, how will you react? Will you take it in and accept it? Will you then study your history and your society with new views being presented? Will you see how everything within these pages is your history and how you are involved in a greater play?

Greetings, I AM Halisarius, your Teacher of your history. Pleiadians are celebrating your life.

You are multidimensional

You are multidimensional,

you hold sacred gifts within you,

of your Star Creators,

who are beautiful,

powerful,

all knowing,

perfect.

If you knew how to awaken,

the powers within you,

you would change your earth,

your very existence,

with your power of love.

If you knew the power within you,

you would desire the great healings,

you would desire the great ways,

for then your love would grow,

into great creator power.

A Komo Ha Halima

Greetings, I AM Halisarius,

Pleiadian Chief Commander & Chief Leader,

Great Leader of the Galactic Federation of Light Society.

Part 26: The power is within you

We welcome you to these pages. You are getting to know us through our words even if you have never met a Pleiadian before reading this book. You already understand much about us. You understand that we have been your teachers a long time ago.

A long time ago, together with other beings from outer space, we taught you and held you in great respect.

Yes, a long, long time ago we were told of your great importance. We were told of your play in the universe.

During the times we were with you, you were aware of your importance but did not realize how significant it was.

This is a story of how you began and how you learned as people.

Do you come from apes or from primates?

We do not have those stories within our records. Do you not think those stories could have been passed down from those who desire you to believe you are limited?

Look at the ape or the relative of the ape. How much intelligence do these beings have? Do they hold the intelligence that we have been discovering together of your ancestors throughout these pages?

Friends, these are stories passed down. These are theories and no matter how much you believe them to be true, you will never find a true link to these beings in your history.

Why? Because there is no truth to it. These stories, if you believe in them, will keep you in limitation and understanding that you are nothing more than an animal.

They do not teach you that you hold magnificent multidimensional powers from the stars within you and that if you learned to access these, your full 12 stranded DNA would become functional.

You could then travel to the stars with your thoughts and through portals of light and find many more dimensions and greater knowledge to bring back to your earth. You would find all the answers are already within you to create your greatness and the greatness of your people.

Imagine if you could access your full DNA and it became functional. Imagine, no more sickness, no more fear, no more pain and suffering on your planet. You would understand the strength and greatness of your very being.

But, and here is a big but, you can only access it and learn the power of yourself through the most powerful force in the universal creation force. That powerful force is love.

How is your love in your society and your world? Do you realize that when you have great love for yourselves, your energy pumps out from your body? Love creates love because you are creating it around you. Have you not noticed smiles returning to you when you give others a smile?

You are using your power of creation by building the love within you.

We discovered this also during our evolution. We discovered the power of love. We had no leaders like you have on your plane. We had no big stories to keep us limited like you have on your plane. We have never known the fear to the degree that you do on your plane.

However, we learned also the power of love. When we came together with the thought and the great power of love, we created new technology to advance our civilizations. We brought these to other planetary beings and helped them also with their technology and advancement.

Understand then, that we know the power of love. Yet, you are able to create stronger love than us as Pleiadians. Within you, you have the power to create the greatest love in the universe.

Do you think beings who desire control and know about the power within you, would not want to stop you from knowing your truth?

What if, you were the key to creating greater peace and unity, not only on your planet, but in all the universal planetary bodies of existences?

What if you were in the middle of a great big theatre play and you were watched by many to see if you could unravel your truth and grasp it, to create change so needed, not only on your planet, but in the entire system of planetary existences?

Do you think you could hold the secret, the greatest secret of all of creation? Would that be possible?

We will allow you to absorb this story and we will return soon.

Greetings, I AM Halisarius, Pleiadian Chief Commander and Great Leader of The Galactic Federation of Light Society.

A Komo Ha Halima

Greetings, I AM Halisarius,

Pleiadian Chief Commander & Chief Leader,

Great Leader of the Galactic Federation of Light Society.

Part 27: The fall of higher consciousness

My responsibility to my race is great. However, I share my responsibility with many Pleiadians and other beings from other planets. We work in unity together and we have gone beyond the arguing for power a long time ago. We have learned from our lessons and hence we have advanced greatly.

We live, as Pleiadians, on different levels of awakening. The younger learn from the Elders who have great spiritual knowledge to share with those not as spiritually advanced. Those of us, who are Elders and are here to teach our Pleiadian civilization and other civilizations like you, have been born enlightened as it were. We knew our purpose from our birth onwards and we remember much of our past history in other past incarnations.

The greatest purpose of all of creation, including your earth and your society, (you are no different) is to find greater love within your heart.

This has been a challenge, not only for your current civilization in the time you are living in, but also for many of your past civilizations in your past history. Many of your people in the past have died at the hands of those who chose not to become love and battled for greed and power.

In other universes there also exist these energies. Not all planets with life have power battles, but some do. These planetary beings who battle, are not yet enlightened. They have still to discover light and love within their hearts.

As you can see from these stories, there are those who have discovered love and those who have not. You are in a time of discovering love for yourself and the power of love.

You were a creation of love and because you separated yourselves so much from the Source of all of life, you lost your sense of wholeness.

Again we say, everything is all an illusion, for in reality you have not lost anything at all. It is all in the way you believe it to be.

Instead of the love frequency fully being implanted within you, to dwell within and help you to grow into your greatness, you received fear energies.

Fear was implanted into your cellular memory and you lost the power of your greater multidimensional bodies. You became denser, more solid, more lost. Your DNA was, as it were, broken and shrunk. It no longer operated itself into the full performance but lost itself during the process.

Fear is a killer. Not only of your physical bodies but of everything you know to be. It destroys you as a person and as a society. You cannot be in the joy and the love if fear exists within you, for you will keep creating your reality based on the fears within you.

Thus, you lost your power. You lost your connection. You lost us. You became sad and lonely and very afraid. You began to believe in the stories of how much of a sinner you were and how you needed to repent to be able to join the heavens. How the stories of burning went through you and limited your very beings.

Today, you may not believe in a fiery hell, or even a heaven. However, within your cellular memories, these belief systems still hold a great deal of pain within you. If we mention a fiery hell, your imagination will take you there and you create it within your mind in an instant. How fearful mankind still is from those stories.

Who would do such a thing to a civilization when so much goodness can be created from the hearts of the pure ones from the light? Who would want to put this beautiful race into so much pain to destroy most of their DNA and put so much fear into their cellular memories to create a slave society of beings?   And why? What is in it for them? Who are they?

These answers will be shared with you in the coming pages. However friends, these are our stories and we are your history record keepers. You are to make up your own mind. How will you take this information? Will you use it for good? Will you put the book away thinking it is just a story and it would make a good script for a movie?

Greetings, I AM Halisarius, Pleiadian Leader, Chief Advisor on the Board of Light Federations.

A Komo Ha Halima

Greetings, I AM Halisarius,
Pleiadian Chief Commander & Chief Leader,
Great Leader of the Galactic Federation of Light Society.

Part 28: We can help you with your issues on your plane

How wonderful it is to be back here with you. How we greet you in our love.

We understand your scenarios on your planet and we wish to help you understand more. I wish to help you with understanding more about yourselves.

You live in the middle of a game. You may not know it. How could you know it? There are no teachings on your planet regarding the game. You cannot go to school to learn about this game or ask a teacher. To learn about your game you must seek the answers from the heavens.

The heavens are rich with knowledge. Far more knowledge than you realize.

We, as Pleiadians in Light, hold the knowledge to transform your planet. We hold the technology to create water, food and electricity on your planet without any hassle or pollution. We can show you how to do this.

Our scientists can help rid your disease on your planet. Imagine, if you could live on a planet like this? You would live your life differently then would you not? Imagine, if we had a cure for every imaginable disease on your plane and taught you how to live in great health?

Is it only a story? If you do not believe that the answers are in the higher realms, why could you possibly hope your people have the answers?

We have allowed time to go by and help you to prove that you need help from your star brothers and star sisters. We have allowed time to go by, to help you understand that you cannot answer all your issues and in order to have solutions to your challenges on your planet, changes are needed within you.

Again, I will bring back the thought of the thought, the power the thought holds. If all of your reality is created with the thought and if all is an illusion, how have your thoughts collectively brought about the situations and challenges in your lives? Do you not then seek to change your thought and your ways so that these challenges disappear from your plane?

Could it possibly happen that you could live in a different way?

We as star beings cannot see why not. However, we have evolved as well and we have seen and witnessed the changes within our civilization and others. You have not yet witnessed these changes, so for you it would be having trust and faith to take these steps.

But then please consider friends, do you have an alternative option? Do you have a choice to choose?

Of course you do. You live in a universe where there is freedom to choose. This unique lesson in your universe gives you the right to choose your own destiny. Would you like to choose to live with your greater understanding of your power within you? Or would you like to choose to live with your pain and suffering?

We cannot take your choice away.

Greetings, I AM Halisarius, Pleiadian friend and teacher. I am here to guide you towards a higher love consciousness.

A Komo Ha Halima

Greetings, I AM Halisarius,

Pleiadian Chief Commander & Chief Leader,

Great Leader of the Galactic Federation of Light Society.

Part 29: Why we cannot join you in the open at this time

If we (we speak for all Star Light beings in existence) chose to live among your people openly, your leaders would destroy us. We would be placed in laboratories and be experimented with. You have done so already to many who entered your space and you are doing so as we are speaking.

Yes, your world leaders know very well that extraterrestrials exist. They have seen us, caught us, experimented on us, taken our fluids, taken our organs while we have been alive and watched our suffering. (When we say 'us,' we mean outsiders of your plane).

Many people are afraid of extraterrestrial visitors from space.

There are some extraterrestrials who are not friendly and desire to understand your biological coding at this time. They desire to understand how strong you are you becoming, what is happening to your DNA at this time and how your coding is changing with your belief systems.

We will not deny this. There are those who are not friendly with you.

We as Pleiadians do not harm people. We come in peace and if you accepted us as your star brothers and star sisters, we would be happy to live on the surface with you, to teach you about the universe.

However, it is not our time yet to come and join you and it is not safe for us to be with you just yet, in the open.

Will we help you understand these other beings who are not friendly towards you?

Yes, you will learn about them through the pages of this book. I will introduce you to some of them. I will show you their power, through the power of our stories.

Again, it is your choice to understand truth behind the stories we tell you. You can learn from them, or reject them.

You are living in a universe of freedom.

It is ultimately your choice.

I will leave you with this thought. Greetings and be in peace. I AM Halisarius, Pleiadian Leader and Chief.

Your inner fear

Your inner fear,

is what you fear greatly.

You fear what you cannot see.

You fear what you do not know.

You fear what you cannot yet touch,

but your greatest fear,

is finding your greater truth,

of the power within you,

of who you are on a greater level,

of how you fell collectively.

Do not fear what you do not know.

Do not fear looking for your greater truth.

Find truth within your heart,

for then you will find,

your glorious, beautiful greater self,

who has always loved you,

who is asking you to return,

to the Great Love within.

A Komo Ha Halima

Greetings, I AM Halisarius,

Pleiadian Chief Commander & Chief Leader,

Great Leader of the Galactic Federation of Light Society.

Part 30: Your discovery about your journey

We greet you and honor you at this time. You have come far into your journey at this time. How we rejoice to be with you and guide you back to where you came from and help you to understand your greatness within you.

Already, you have discovered much. You have discovered about your illusions and how everything you think you see and experience is but an illusion of your mind. Everything is a game, a game of understanding, a game of decision making, a game of learning to walk forward.

Here, I would like to teach the thought of letting go of your past pain.

Already I discussed earlier how important it is to let go of the pain of your past wars. How you are holding on to too much pain of the past because of your fears that it may happen again. We say to you, continue and it will happen; worse than you have experienced before. During the last few decades alone hundreds of thousands of your people have died in ways of catastrophes and at the hands of your dictators. Yet, because it was not involving the world on a large scale, you forget about it so easy.

People can be monstrous to each other. Look at how much you poisoned yourselves and the earth during your war you had in Vietnam. Many have fallen, been poisoned at their dictator's hands. You are still poisoning and harming yourselves today. You do not understand the harm you have caused yourselves and all species on earth.

Your earth is out of balance at this moment and it concerns us because we know and understand its purpose. It was created in perfection with the perfect intention to help a species, a race discover its freedom; a freedom that is rare in the Universal Bodies of Creation.

With that freedom you discovered your hate and your pollution. You have pained the earth, and although the warning signs continue to show on your earth, people as a whole are not doing anything about it. Yes, there are those who care for the earth so much.

Many of our readers of this book are healers of the earth. They care very much and are wondering what they can do about healing your earth.

You will learn much. Please do not think we blame you personally. Again, your situation has been set up deliberately to make you fail in the purpose you set out to be here on this earth for, by beings not of love. That greater purpose you have was to find the ultimate love for each other and yourselves as Divine Beings.

Yes, you desired to explore love. At the beginning of your Soul Family Light creation, you, as Family of Light, believed that love could eliminate all challenges that would come to the earth. You discovered it well before setting foot on your planet. You had plans, knowing full well the possible scenarios your human society could bring.

We will teach you much more in the following pages. Please friends, open your minds to the greatness that you came here for. Give some thought and consideration as to why you came here to this planet. Not only to experience great love, but to create such an incredible force of love on your planet to wipe out any possible darkness that could infiltrate upon earth.

Your history proved that it turned out otherwise. The darkness did come and throughout time you forgot about the greatness of light and where you came from. The darkness brought much pain and war upon your planet.

A Komo Ha Halima

Greetings, I AM Halisarius,
Pleiadian Chief Commander & Chief Leader,
Great Leader of the Galactic Federation of Light Society.

Part 31: Your history is our history

We as Pleiadians are a much older race than you. We evolved a long, long time ago. We have not always existed on our planets. We looked for other homes when our planet was invaded many millions of years ago and then settled on the Pleiades.

Many wars have happened in the universal bodies of space. You would be surprised at the extent of destruction. I wish to instruct you on some of the damage that has been done in our past.

As you know we enjoy sharing good stories. We enjoy sharing stories with you because it helps you to reason more. We wish to help you expand your mind. As you expand your mind, your brain expands because your brain breathes in more life when it thinks and it becomes excited. Your brain is an organ, constantly growing and expanding and breathing.

There are beings, as we have already discussed, that do not desire peace and love in the universe. They created large challenges which we will discuss later on throughout this book. I wish you not to be too impatient for information as we will answer many of your questions at this time.

Why? This is because now it is your time of understanding so that you can make a conscious decision.

Your Archangels and Divine Beings are partnering up with people more on the surface on your planet because it is time to understand what has happened in your past and what you are involved with.

How can you understand what is going on if no one explains to you the game and the battle?

You are involved in the largest game and battle in history.

You may say, 'Us? Really? But I do not understand. I do not comprehend the war and the battle.'

I, Halisarius, am honored to teach you about the universe and about my experiences and our history together.

Your history is also our history. Your pain is also our pain. Your experiences are also our experiences. Please understand that we consider you our family and we are also your family.

Let us look at some of the tragedies in the past. Why? Is it to bring you fear? No. Fear is not what we desire to introduce to you at all. We desire to help you understand how to come out of the fear. But your truth must be told before you can work towards coming out of the fear.

Fear exists in the mind when the unknown is present. You realize this very much do you not? Your mind will make you fearful if you do not understand a situation in your life. If you are unsure about the happening of future events, you create fear within your mind.

Hence, the same with these writings and teachings. We wish to help you understand to take fear away.

You all know terrible events have happened in your history. We ask you, are you ready to understand what has happened? Or will you stay closed to this knowledge?

Greetings and be in peace. I AM Halisarius, Pleiadian Chief Leader.

The great heavens are rejoicing

The great heavens are rejoicing,

the Angels are singing their great songs,

to the people upon the earth.

Their voices are loud and clear,

'Rejoice all of creation,

for the Great Light has returned,

to show the ways to the Great Love,

to awaken the people to love,

to show the way to the greater path.'

Light brings love, peace, wisdom,

guidance, answers, truth, joy, healing.

All you have been seeking,

is now able to be received,

into your Sacred Loving Heart,

your Golden Heart of Love.

A Komo Ha Halima

Greetings, I AM Halisarius,
Pleiadian Chief Commander & Chief Leader,
Great Leader of the Galactic Federation of Light Society.

Part 32: The prophecy of Light

I made a vow when I left planet earth a long, long time ago. I vowed to you, to the people of planet earth, to all the Archangels in the Power of the Light and all the Glory, that I would return with truth and that one day, when it was time, the records of history of earth would be told.

No man could wipe out the entire history as they have tried to do many times.

Even though many of your leaders have wiped and destroyed much of your history, much of it still exists. It is precious information. It holds keys to your universe, to who is who and who is ruling which planet and where it all began.

Much of what you have been told is lies. Much of what you have been led to believe are false leads.

Your leaders are frightened that you will understand your true history. They are frightened of you understanding truth. Do not worry; they cannot do anything with this information. By the time they know this information is out to the people, it will be too late. Nothing can be done.

The Archangels have spoken, 'Halisarius, it is time to bring your history to the people. Share with the people your knowledge through your Channel and Blue Star. The prophecy must now be fulfilled.'

And so it is that I am transmitting these words. Words held back, even from many of my own race, to bring them to the light now.

Why? Because this information is precious and it must stay precious.

You may question to find out what its importance is.

You are about to discover the wars, the secrets, the reason for your planet. I will introduce you to some of the beings not desiring to have peace and love on your planet.

Why? Why am I giving you this information? Is it to bring fear into your mind?

Friends, the fear already exists. It lives within your bones and every cell that you have. You have feared these beings for many thousands upon many thousands of years. I cannot bring the fear. Perhaps when you read these words, you will remember and that will frighten some of you.

But please know, you are able to bring an end to all of it. This is what your leaders know and have feared for so long.

A long time ago a prophecy was foretold:

'Darkness will come upon mankind. It will bring an end to the light that the people know well. The people will grope in the dark for a time, not knowing where light has gone.

They will cry out, 'Where is Light?'

Confusion will be upon earth. People will be swayed within their hearts from here to there like the waves of the oceans.

Look to the heavens and see the signs of the end of times. Light will be restored and the people will be in light once more. They will be led to refreshing waters and their thirst will be quenched. They will be fattened with good news and their salvation will be theirs. They will claim their victory. The earth will rejoice once again and the past will never be repeated ever again.'

Please friends, when you are in fear on your planet, meditate upon this prophecy. Dwell your thoughts upon it and pray for your salvation and your truth to be shown to you. Each time you dwell upon it the powers of the heavens will bless you and help you to become stronger with light that you are.

This prophecy, the more it is uttered on the surface of the earth, the greater its strength and power. Use it well. It is precious to each and every one of you who desires greatness.

This prophecy was not to be uttered through times of darkness. Whoever spoke of light was destroyed by the deadened hearts not of light. These people of light were tormented and tortured. Many were hung, burned, stoned, beheaded, killed and eaten by beasts. Many starved for years until they died of pestilence that struck their flesh. Their flesh may have suffered but their spirit stayed strong.

Why am I sharing this with you? To help you understand, that through the times of darkness upon earth, many still had great faith, determined to believe in the Great Spirit of the Divine One.

Are you awakening yet? Are you remembering yet?

I will return soon.

Greetings, I AM Halisarius, Pleiadian Leader, Chief Commander of our Pleiadian Civilization.

A Komo Ha Halima

Greetings, I AM Halisarius,
Pleiadian Chief Commander & Chief Leader,
Great Leader of the Galactic Federation of Light Society.

Part 33: Revealed – History of Mars

As you have gathered from our stories, you are not the first planet to have pain and suffering. However, you are the first planet to experience many energies that are new to the game of life.

Again, I am opening your mind with my stories.

Here I am going to tell you a story. This is a story that occurred a long time ago. Well before you were created and came to be in existence. You are much older than you realize as you will find out on your discoveries. Much is yet to be discovered on your earth. I am here to open your mind. You can reflect upon the rest.

A planet in your Milky Way system, Mars, has been in great pain since a long time ago.

Allow me to introduce you to Mars the way it was. You would not recognize Mars at this moment as I explain to you what it was like. In your imagination you can see the way it was.

Mars was alive. It was alive with vegetation, treasures, water. It was rich. It was beautiful. It was a loving place to bring up children. The people on Mars lived well. They lived together and worked together. Small arguments happened every so often, but nothing too much. In general, much harmony existed between the people.

The people who inhabited Mars were stronger than you. The men were larger than you. They were kind to each other and they worked hard. They worshipped the Gods and they had many traditions. They had their own living book as well, like you have your Bible and other 'Living Books.'

They were visited by other beings from the 'skies' as they called it. 'Flying in their spaceships,' as you would say. Much intelligence was shared with them. Martians were kind and hospitable beings. They would take anyone into their home in exchange for a gift or a service.

This is the way they lived. They only knew to live in that way. At that time they did not know of slavery. They did not know of unjust. They had no courtrooms. There was no killing and no bloodshed.

You would call it, 'Utopia,' for it was.

Martians were peaceful and deeply spiritual beings. They had their traditions and temples. They set out time for worship. They believed their creators, (other beings from other galaxies) were their gods and they worshipped them and made many offerings.

Here I would like to pose a question to you. Please consider my last part of my story. Can you see similarities on earth with the worship and the offerings?

One day, when it was a fine day, the people of Mars worked hard as usual. They were happy as they always were.

Then, space beings arrived in their golden chariots. The Martians saw them. Thinking they were the Gods, they bowed down before them as these beings exited their golden chariots.

These were not good beings. They did not want to help them. They were after the gold and the treasures of Mars for their weapons and evolution to destroy and take over other planets with life.

These beings, took Martians as their prisoners, placed chains upon them and killed any who did not want to obey. They whipped many and took the little ones away from their mothers.

As you can imagine, this was terrifying for them. Mars was a peaceful place before this time and now it had turned into this terrible scene.

The men were enslaved and were used to dig in the mines. These beings from space had many other chariots from their planets coming to them with expansive technology. Technology you are not familiar with at this moment in your time.

This technology could dig out whole mountains. They knew exactly where the treasures were hidden and they used the Martian men to dig out their treasures.

The pain, the agony, the killings that took place you could not imagine. The beings of Mars wept and cried together at the hands of these beings who had no goodness, no mercy and no heart. They prayed for answers to come but no answers came.

The dead were not buried but burnt so no remainders would ever be found. No proof of its history. No trace.

The women, who were beautiful and handsome, were raped, tortured and used to create their babies. They then killed the women when there was no more use for them, as these beings, these dark vultures, did not have any respect for the goddess aspect.

The story does not end there. Mars was mined. All its beauty was stolen. Energetically it died as soon as these vultures entered its atmosphere.

The men of Mars mourned their women. They hated the offspring these beings produced with their women. Their offspring were not like the Martians but they were bullies. They grew to be large. They destroyed anything in their way. They took out trees like it was a child's game. They stamped on the ground and the ground would shake. They even killed many of their own fathers. (Their fathers being the ones without light within their hearts.)

Their offspring, hundreds and hundreds of them, became too many; even for the dark beings. They grew into a large army. They planned together. They warred against their fathers. They killed the Martians who were left because they were considered weak compared to these bullies.

Everything on Mars was destroyed. The bullies eventually died also. There was no more food. There was nothing. Mars was desolate. These offspring were not intelligent. You would call them zombies walking on a dead planet. They could not think how to use technology or to connect too well to life. All they knew was to fight; to kill and destroy.

Sadly, this is how Mars ended.

We bring this to your knowledge because we understand that mankind is incredibly interested and curious in Mars and what this planet has to offer you.

We tell you, there are still many treasures left on Mars that would benefit you greatly. However, here we will also give you a warning.

The Martians have not left. After their death, they travelled to another dimension and they are now, still to this day, the Keepers of Mars. Their vow to each other is that no one will ever harm Mars again.

Please understand Mars was their beloved planet. They still care for it. They still mourn their planet. They are still angry with their history. They will guard it at any cost.

Please do not investigate Mars as accidents will happen. Do not go to great investigations. It is a planet not to be touched. PLEASE LEAVE IT ALONE. We only say this with great love in our hearts for you.

We have given you a history lesson and a look into what some of these dark beings are like. Yes, we call them vultures. They take what is not theirs to have, without caring and love. They walk without hearts. These beings watch their prey, study them and then attack.

If you looked deep into the quiet

If you looked,

deep into the quiet,

you would find your greater truth,

of all existence.

You would then begin to change,

your thoughts and actions,

your belief patterns.

You would look upwards.

You would look at the flows,

within the universal cycle.

You would not look at others,

what they believe in,

for when you know,

how the universe works,

you would carry the great strength,

to see your greater truth within,

because you carry your truth within.

of all of creation.

A Komo Ha Halima

Greetings, I AM Halisarius,
Pleiadian Chief Commander & Chief Leader,
Great Leader of the Galactic Federation of Light Society.

Part 34: The numbing of mankind

We are happy you stayed with us and you are continuing to read these pages. We want to give you many lessons and teachings.

Again like I have said many times in this book of pages, we are telling you stories. Is there any truth to these stories?

What would be the point if there was not? Do you feel the truth in these stories? Do you see similarities or understand the truths within these stories? We allow you to be the decision maker.

At this time, I am asking you not to be too alarmed with the stories of Mars. I do not think that many of our readers will however be too shocked.

Why do I say this friends?

Because, mankind, has by and large been numbed to pain. How have you been numbed? You may refuse to believe this. You may even laugh at this comment as if I was a good old friend of yours and I was telling you a joke.

Yes, you have been numbed, numbed to reality and to pain.

How?

Your television screens are a good example. You turn on your television screens and feed your minds with murders and killings. You have opened your minds to science fiction stories with the terrible stories of what aliens may look like and may do to you.

You have been trained to turn off your senses and distrust anyone from the universe.

Are you aware of this we ask you?

We ask you this question now. If I was going to say a space ship was going to land in your garden at 2.00p.m., tomorrow afternoon, what would you expect?

Would you expect to see an alien like you have been exposed to on your television screens? Would you have weapons in case it would somehow try and destroy you? Would you be ready to call in your armies and police to hunt it down and take it to a laboratory to be dissected?

Or, would you be open minded enough to welcome this friend from out of space.

Of course, here we say to you, be selective. There are the goodies and the baddies, like in any culture.

We are far and wide different species. One species may be here to help you and another species would love to destroy you. Even beings from the same species may have different intentions.

Be always selective and be wise.

However, I have opened your mind again. Have you been numbed to pain?

Yes, you have. How could you have not been numbed? Your whole society has been based on understanding pain and slavery. It has been based on understanding unnecessary killings. Not only in war times, but every day you hear it on your news.

How frightened many of you are. Again, we say, be careful of what you fear, for everything within your mind you bring it into being.

Here is another question I will pose to you for your greater awareness. Who put the fear into your mind? Could you perhaps have experienced similar experiences as the people did on Mars? Could the same beings have come here to earth? Could it be that where Mars failed because of their offspring, they came to earth with different techniques?

If so, did they succeed in their plans? Or did they fail?

A Komo Ha Halima, I AM Halisarius, Pleiadian Teacher, Leader and Chief Commander.

You are not alone

You are not alone,

in the Grand Universe,

of all of existence.

You have many star brothers,

and star sisters living,

celebrating your life together.

They are keenly watching,

keenly observing,

keenly recording,

patiently waiting,

to see the path you will discover.

They praise you for being upon the earth,

to play in your dimensions.

They call to you,

'Awaken to your inner light.'

Loudly they say to you,

'Rejoice, for the Great Light is here.

to guide you home.'

A Komo Ha Halima

Greetings, I AM Halisarius,

Pleiadian Chief Commander & Chief Leader,

Great Leader of the Galactic Federation of Light Society.

Part 35: Learning to not be trapped in your world

By now you will have gathered, that not only do I understand existence and your history, but I also am a great teacher.

Some of you will enjoy these pages. You are opening your mind much. You are learning much. Others among you will be thinking, 'Hurry up. We want the juicy parts.'

We desire to teach you, to help you understand how you can make a difference in your world. Yes, I could wrap my story in five or so pages, but do you not desire to understand our teachings in between? To us as Pleiadians in the Light, we are also great Light Workers and Light Shiners, as we are often called, and our teachings are more important for your enlightenment than your history.

However, history has many precious lessons to offer to you too. After all, it is good to know about your past so that you are prepared for your future.

Prepared for what you may ask?

Again, these are questions that will be discovered by those who are faithful to these pages and follow these lessons.

Do not always be impatient for there is a time and a place for everything. That is a saying of yours is it not?

In our language, if I may translate it, we say to our young ones; 'Young ones, have faith that everything has a time and a season. A season for love. A season for sleep. A season for the sun rising. A season for learning and a season for rest.'

It is perfect. You must always work with your seasons and never strive too much ahead because then your wishes will not work out as well.

Yes, we teach that everything is created in the mind. It is true. And yes, you can create all your greatness in your mind as well, because as you create the energy within your inner eye, so it will also be. However, there is also a Divine Purpose for everything. Everything in its own time. Time has perfection.

People on your planet desire everything at once. When you think or see something, many of you become impulsive. Why? It is because the eyes can trap you. Do not always believe everything you see with your eyes. Your whole society is based on trapping your eyes. Everything around you looks sparkly and shiny. Your world is about have, have, have. It has forgotten about giving, instead it has become about the having.

What has been the consequence of being trapped by your eyes? Many of you have become in severe debt over the trap of the eyes.

You have forgotten a vital lesson that is plain to everyone and everyone knows it. You must not fall in the trap of what you see and hear. First consider, do you need to have it? How much will you enjoy it? Or will you be gathering the treasures that you do not need to have?

How much heavier will your load be? How much more will you have to carry?

We on the Pleiadian Realms, live differently than you. Our technology is greater, but so will yours be when you learn to live in greater love together. We can also teach you much with your technology once the time comes.

We live lighter however. We do not have the fancy things you have. We are more with nature. We play with light and energy. We keep ourselves occupied with our mind. We play with our mind. We draw and write. We visit and experiment.

Our children are greatly educated. Before they begin our great schools, parents already know their children's gifts. Our children are incredibly gifted as you can imagine. Some are highly mathematical, others are incredible healers, others can draw magically and others are spectacular with mind control and telepathy.

We all have these gifts, but like you, we have great talent among us. In our education system our children are brought up in a system that is built around building their talents.

Our school system is not like yours. We do not have a general stream where the children need to discuss and know certain things, like you do. Yes, our children are highly educated, but they are educated in the field of their talents. They all understand our rules and governments. They understand the universal history. They understand much about you.

But here let me illustrate a nine year old Pleiadian boy. His brain is greatly developed, like all of our Pleiadian children. He can read encyclopedias at a speed that is faster than your fastest speed reader. His mathematical knowledge exceeds far greater than Albert Einstein. His scientific explorations are magnificent. He has built a space ship in the shed of his father, using computer technology of his father, knowing the software, using mind control and this space ship can fly at astronomical speeds.

This is a nine year old boy. Not all our children are as talented as he is, however. I am pointing out this example to help you understand the education of our young ones.

For them to vegetate in front of a PlayStation or television all day, watching programs that 'numb' the mind, would be out of the question. If they watch any programs, if they participate in any game, it is highly active, highly stimulating and it will help them to accelerate in their lives.

Yes, we are high strivers. However, we are differently built than you also. Our brain's speed is faster than yours. We are not human either. We live in a higher dimension, although we are able to look like a human when we come to your planet, as we often have in the past and sometimes still do, and will much more into the future. We do not have blood like you, but we do have a fluid that runs through us to keep us healthy and strong.

We stay young for many, many years. We can become hundreds of years if we wish and some of us can become older, depending on our evolution and our process of purpose.

We are spiritually aware and are highly telepathic, not only with each other, but also with Spirit, and we work together as one.

Later, through these pages, I will introduce you to The Galactic Federation from my perspective, because, after all, it is my story.

We, as a race are a part of this federation, and I, Halisarius, am one of the Leaders and Chief Advisors of the Galactic Federation. Our job on the Galactic Federation of Light is highly important in the Scheme of the Universe.

Greetings, I AM Halisarius, Pleiadian Leader. I constantly guide many teams of Pleiadians on missions to awaken the people of the earth to love consciousness.

Your earth is alive

Your earth is alive,
thriving with living memories,
of your ancient past,
and of your greatest future.
It stores all knowledge of life,
for time does not exist,
all is happening now.
There are many gateways,
many secrets,
many dimensions,
waiting to unfold for you.
The time is coming,
when you will find them,
and you will tap into,
the greater dimensions,
and then you will see collectively,
that all answers already exist.
Awaken.

A Komo Ha Halima

Greetings, I AM Halisarius,

Pleiadian Chief Commander & Chief Leader,

Great Leader of the Galactic Federation of Light Society.

Part 36: Your earth is alive

We hope you enjoy reading these pages. You have learned much have you not? I have shared with you much about our realms of existence through these pages. Perhaps a little by a little, but you have learned much about us.

We desire to become more of your friends. Many of you are reaching out to us and we are happy for that. You will find a friend that is your Pleiadian friend and this friend will guide you to greater knowledge of our Pleiadian realms.

The beauty you have on your planet is very precious in the Universal Bodies of Planetary Existences. Your treasures upon the earth are greatly admired, and hence, your treasures like Mars have also been plundered.

Does this mean that earth will never return to its original beauty? No, for you all hold a secret within you that can balance your heart of your earth, but you must learn to align yourselves with your planet first.

Your earth is not only just a planet. You have just a couch you sit on. You have just a floor you stand on. Your car is just a car that takes you from one destination to another. You may be proud of your couch, your floor or your car. You may decide that these things you own are necessary, which they are. We will not dispute this. However, they are simply things you own. They do not hold a great importance other than they are the things you own.

You may refute this thought.

The earth is not 'just' a thing. She is not like your floor, or your car, or your stereo, your fancy big television, or your latest computer.

She is alive and breathes, like you do. You may be surprised. We have done great investigations on your planet. We understand your planet better than your greatest scientists do, although you may also refute this.

We hope you understand this in the kindness that we feel for you. We are lighthearted beings. We are friendly and we never mean any harm.

Let us continue with our discussion. We desire to help you understand your earth better because she is a large part of you, of your race, of your children, of your history, of all of history.

As you follow our stories through these pages, you will understand more about the importance of your planet and how special humankind is.

Here is another thought to help you expand your mind. Have you ever considered that planet earth was never meant for your species as you are today? That it was created for a different race but because of the events that happened, you came to be in existence?

Perhaps you are thinking of the Ape, or a relation of the Ape, or some Primate.

However, we are not referring to those species. We are referring to a race with high intelligence which looked like you but far from what you are today. As they were and are your ancestors, you have the capability to open to their gifts and potential. You still have their gifts waiting to be awakened.

That thought will stir your mind.

Back to our story of the earth. The earth is a jewel in the Universal Bodies of Galaxies and all its systems. It holds a special force. It holds a special secret that allows much growth to come upon her, much more than many other planets in existence.

We will discuss this also throughout the pages. All these are stories untold until now. You must be excited to understand so much. How these stories have remained hidden for so long. You are about to discover much about you, your existence and how you came to be.

Your earth has dimensions many of you have discovered. Many spiritual seekers understand these dimensions well.

You are yet to discover very important dimensions. These dimensions hold a life force within her to restore all its energies back to the earth.

When you are strong enough, and you are able to tap into these higher dimensions together, you will restore paradise back on your planet.

Along the way, you will have much guidance and help. Please do not try to run ahead of yourselves and go through painstaking effort to try and force it to happen. Like we said earlier throughout these pages, when it is the time and the season it will happen because Divine Timing is of utmost importance. Be patient.

The earth has chakra centers also just like you do. These chakra centers are powerful. They are sensitive. At this moment, her base chakra is not working much at all. Her understanding of who she is and why she is here is in deep pain.

You are able to help her by helping her remember who she is. Tell her she was once beautiful and awaken her to her beauty. When many of you do this together, when she hears the love you have for her, how she will be restored once again, how the pain will come away from her and how never again she will have to repeat her pain, she will awaken.

At this moment, though she is alive, she is very much asleep also.

Why the earthquakes if she is asleep? Why the storms?

Precisely why, it is because she is asleep. She does not feel the love of the people. She only feels the pain of your presence, your wars, your pollution and destruction, the mining, the oil leaving her veins within her and other treasures leaving her. She is asleep and she dares not wake up in case she is bombarded with more pain.

This is why you must communicate with her and ask her to wake up. Talk nicely to your earth. Feel the earth's heartbeat because she has one. Sing with her heart beat. She will love hearing your song.

She will awaken when you awaken to how powerful she is and to who she is. I will leave you with this lesson and will allow you to absorb the information.

Greetings, I AM Halisarius as always, Pleiadian Leader and your teacher, and throughout these pages, your guide.

A Komo Ha Halima

Greetings, I AM Halisarius,
Pleiadian Chief Commander & Chief Leader,
Great Leader of the Galactic Federation of Light Society.

Part 37: Technology – Freedom or Frustration?

How happy we are to have returned here to these spaces to help you in your life. You are progressing within yourselves and desiring to understand yourself further and you are

looking for ways to become more greatly aware of all things that are around you.

Much you do not understand. Much is confusing to you. We will try and help you through your maze within your lives.

Keeping your life simple is one of the greatest challenges for you in your society. Everything you touch almost seems to have its own complications and frustrations.

Here, I am going to ask you a question to help you become more aware of your society and how it is run. Did you know that much technology around you is to make you feel frustrated and keep you feeling you are not achieving?

Do you understand this brothers and sisters? You, as a whole, seem to think you are progressing much forward and yes you are. You are creating much of your technology for your progress.

However, your leaders do not desire you to think too smartly so they keep you in limitation far more than you realize.

The frustration, irritation about your technology alone, creates a great fear in your society. You fear your society more greatly than you realize. Everything you touch has rays and many of these rays are there to numb your mind, to keep you away from your true senses.

Do you understand this dear friends?

You take your microwave for example. A microwave helps you to cook faster does it not?

At what consequence?

We are not saying eliminate them altogether, however we are saying please be careful with them. Do not overuse them and please do not get too close to them while they are in use.

These rays come into your brain. Your brain desires to grow and understand. Your brain desires to be sharpened every day. Your brain is alive. When it is alive with a happy frequency, it grows and expands.

However, when it is constantly bombarded by your waves, and you have many, you become numb with understandings. You do not truly connect within yourselves anymore.

We are simply pointing out some of the traps of your society. Has it brought you greater freedom, or frustration? You will find that it has given you both.

Frustration is one of the greatest ways to keep disrupting who you are. Even when you visit your store because you desire to have some technology, you are bombarded with choices. It is far from easy.

Frustration makes you feel unintelligent, bombarded and at times angry.

Could this be another tactic to keep you limited? I will leave you with this thought.

A Komo Ha Halima, Greetings, I AM Halisarius, Pleiadian Chief and Leader.

What is truth?

What is truth?

What will you discover?

What stories have you heard?

Do you believe your teachers?

Study its foundation.

Return to the very beginning.

Return to the beginning of time,

of all of creation,

in the space ,

of all of existence,

to find your greater truth.

Find your heart within your truth,

for you are part of all existence,

you are part of all that is.

Find your truth within your heart.

You will find the answers,

have always been within you.

A Komo Ha Halima

Greetings, I AM Halisarius,

Pleiadian Chief Commander & Chief Leader,

Great Leader of the Galactic Federation of Light Society.

Part 38: Fear and control through time

We come to you in peace and we are here to help you understand yourselves more. We are here to help you understand why you are here and what your greater purpose is and what the Divine Plan is about.

Many of you are wondering all these questions. At times you have many questions that you do not have the courage to ask.

Again, does it bring a feeling of being unintelligent with fear of speaking and then somehow failing?

Friends, please understand that to speak your questions is one of the greatest gifts you can give to yourself and another, for then you will reach true understanding.

You, as a people, feel at times lost and ashamed to be lost. We say, but this is how you have been brought up in your society. You have not been brought up to keep asking.

Your leaders have much to answer. These stories we tell you go back many, many tens of thousands of years ago.

In this story, I want to take you back to a time several hundred thousand years ago.

You may ask if this is possible that you have been here that long. Our records go back over 400 thousand years ago when you first came here to this planet, along with many other star beings, supporting you and teaching you about yourselves.

That may seem a long time ago to you. If we told you, your existence dates back further than this still, would you have trouble identifying with this?

We ask you why you have trouble with this thought, since everything in existence, in its creation, is billions and billions of years old.

You are a young civilization still.

At the beginning of your existence you existed in perfection, before the destruction of the greater consciousness, before mankind fell upon its darkness, before other beings interrupted with your perfection.

Some people think that you have only existed for 7,000 or so years. Again, this is the limited mind with the limited viewpoint. You are far greater than you believe yourselves to be. Much evidence has been found of an ancient culture, far older than you have believed it to be, but much of it has been destroyed and hidden, in case you find your true nature.

The ones who seek control say, 'It is better to leave the people in the fear and the limitation rather than to find the truth.'

It is the same when the man Jesus was on the earth. The stories you read in the Bible are far different to what truly happened. Jesus was a good man. He knew the light and he taught love and light. He desired to help people reach the light. He was a good channel of light and spoke with a heart of love and light, which is what he was.

He healed, he spoke truth and he showed many the way of light.

However, there were many against him. He took the power away from the leaders in those days. Jesus' following became big. Jesus never claimed to be the Messiah. He never claimed to be their King.

He was tortured and persecuted because of his light. Why? Too many people began to rebel against their religious leaders. Too many people disowned their old ways of thinking and instead learned their own freedom.

Jesus stood for freedom. He always taught to find freedom within.

Was he a rebel, like many people believe today? No. He was a fighter for freedom. He was a good man.

Years and years later the leaders changed the records. They burned and destroyed much and changed it. They turned the story into Jesus, the Holy Man. They changed the story to make people believe they were sinners and that he was their Savior and hereby making people believe they needed to be controlled. They introduced hell and heaven, creating a great fear and turned people away from light.

Why? Because your leaders throughout history have always desired control and power as they do today.

To keep you in fear and control means you will never discover your true potential.

Yes, back in Jesus' day, the leaders needed to persecute and torture Jesus to make an example of him to the crowd. They wanted their control back.

Please consider this thought. I will return back later.

Greetings, I AM Halisarius, Pleiadian Teacher for your planet and for our people.

A Komo Ha Halima

Greetings, I AM Halisarius,

Pleiadian Chief Commander & Chief Leader,

Great Leader of the Galactic Federation of Light Society.

Part 39: Early existence on earth

I have returned and we bring our blessings with us to your planet.

At this stage you may be wondering what to do with the information we have presented to you within these pages.

At this time, we desire you to open your mind and to begin to understand your history and how you are placed within the game.

Let us go back a few hundred thousand years ago. This was a time very special to many of us as Pleiadian Beings and very special to many other Star Beings also.

We all knew this earth was going to become very special in the hearts of many. We longed for the exciting adventures ahead.

Like I have mentioned earlier in this book, this earth became alive with its richness from other beings and much of their DNA was implanted in many of the species brought here to this earth.

Imagine the excitement. Imagine the planning. Imagine how the seas were filled with life, and how happy everything was. All of creation was good and in the eyes of all the beings who were part of its creation, and your original creators, it was good and perfect.

You may ask yourself, all the beings who were part of its creation? Not one Supreme Being? How is that?

Again, many of our stories may surprise you. We will come back to that very question in our later pages as you will begin to unravel your history and the reasons for your creation.

Much is yet to be discovered our dear ones of the earth.

Yes, many beings have taken part in your creation. It was grand and it was beautiful. Many Star Beings in the light desired to take a grand part in its creation.

We came here to take part in the greatest play in the universe. Your universe was created where freedom was the game and freedom of living the choice. How would the game play out? How would the choices be made?

Your ancestors, who came to your earth first, were perfect in every way. They were playful. Their bodies were not as dense as yours are today. They looked like you but they were not like you. They did not age like you do. They lived a long time and they could leave the earth at any time. There was no time restriction.

They were busy however. Their job was to create beauty and love on your planet. They created flowers, each with a different vibration from their star frequency.

Does this surprise you? Why do you think your flowers make you smile and why do you think you are attracted to your flowers?

Your trees and all of vegetation were given to you especially for your healing and your love.

Yes, these beings knew a large game was to be played out. No one knew exactly how it would play out and in what way it would affect the earth and her people upon her.

They stayed there many years. They lived together. They could travel back to the stars and back to earth. They gave earth many gifts. Many crystals came from the stars.

Many crystals were placed into the earth because each of the crystals carries a vibration for your healing and to keep the earth strong. Many of them are passageways for you and for Spirit to connect. Many of them were given to you to remember your true identity.

No sickness existed. No fear or pain. These were not part of their play at this time. They had a perfect DNA and they were coded to be strong and powerful. Their spiritual gifts were immense and they created life together, in beauty and in love. They desired to discover their magnificence together. They were completely unlimited and their potential not yet discovered.

Greetings, I AM Halisarius, Pleiadian Chief Leader. Federation Guidance Counselor.

A Komo Ha Halima

Greetings, I AM Halisarius,

Pleiadian Chief Commander & Chief Leader,

Great Leader of the Galactic Federation of Light Society.

Part 40: You are shielded from your true identity

We come in peace and we welcome you to these pages. Have you considered many thoughts here? You may have many questions. You may consider where the evidence has gone of these perfect people. Why has no evidence been found?

Please keep in mind, we are relating to you a game that was played out hundreds of thousands of years ago and there have been good reasons to keep it from you.

Why? Again, we would like to remind you this was to shield you from your truth. Imagine if you knew what your truth was. You would know how to restore your powers. You would not listen to your leaders like you do at present because you would understand the game. You would not fear them any longer and as a result they would lose their game of controlling you.

I will return back to my story of the earth soon. I desire to take you into the universe now and change the scene. You do not mind stories do you? Stories expand your mind. Expanding your mind is good. It helps you to understand more.

As you have already gathered from these pages, your universe is vast. You live in an illusional universe. You cannot move beyond what you see and know about at present because you are not permitted to go outside of your boundaries. You do not understand the vastness of the universe.

Why? Because their game is to keep you limited and shielded from your true identity. It is also to protect ourselves and many other Star Beings.

If you knew the treasures, the possibilities, the power you could have on other planets, you would be like a virus to us like you are a virus to your planet earth at this present moment. Your anger and greed would overtake you and you would start warring on our planets.

We wonder if you understand our messages. We wish to bring peace and love to your planet. We are teaching you, in order to understand the greatness and vastness of all that is, you must change your ways from the greed and the anger into peace and love. Peace and love is important in the universe, far more important than you realize.

Greetings, I AM Halisarius, Pleiadian Leader and Teacher.

A Komo Ha Halima

Greetings, I AM Halisarius,
Pleiadian Chief Commander & Chief Leader,
Great Leader of the Galactic Federation of Light Society.

Part 41: The game of all existence

There are many universes. It is unimaginably large. We are time travelers, zone jumpers, space discoverers. The amount we as Pleiadian Discoverers have discovered is only small compared to the vastness there is out there.

We are trying to help you understand the vastness of the universes.

Your universe, in all reality, is flat. That might surprise you to hear that. You have universes above you and underneath you. Layer upon layer upon layer. Yet, in your galaxy you may not think that. You may look into your telescopes and not see that.

Why? To keep you away from other universes at this particular moment. We, as a large array of Star Beings working with Divine Will, are incredibly particular about who comes and who does not come to visit us. We are able to shut portals and open portals. When it is time you will discover more.

Please do not be frustrated.

Many games exist in the universe. We all have different rules and understandings. Some of the games and laws are about technology and evolution, others are about understanding love and joy, others are about learning sound and frequency, others are about having a holiday in between incarnations.

As you can see, the universe is enormous and the plays are also vast. Your game in your universe is about freedom of choice, freedom to serve and freedom to live.

What would you choose? Who would you choose to believe? What would you choose to worship?

These were questions that would be raised and in time would be answered on your planet.

In the Universe, there are many planetary star beings who desire love and light. They understand what it means to have love and light and desire more than anything to work with it. Their technology is great and they are doing much for many other brothers and sisters on their planet and on other planets to expand their evolutionary path of wisdom.

Then there are the 'others' as we call them. They are not evil or truly dark but they have to learn to grow to live in light.

These beings however have a great place in the universe also. They help us, who are the Family of Light, to understand the shadows and the dark. How else can we know light when only light exists? For light to become stronger, dark must also exist, side by side with the light.

As you know, this is very true.

Here I will reveal the Divine Plan. Many people on your plane have wondered what the Divine Plan is, and how is it you fit into the Divine Plan?

The Divine Plan is about the Sanctification of the One who is the Rightful Source of All of Creation. The Divine Plan is about unifying all and bringing all beings in line with the Higher Will of the One Source of All of Creation.

This may surprise many of you.

The sanctification process has been the greatest and most important task in all of history since the battle of light and dark began, a long, long time ago.

Why would that surprise you? Many of you understand the battle between dark and light to be here on your planet. Would you also not realize how big potentially it could be in the vastness of all the universes? Imagine for a moment, armies from all planets gathering themselves together for a battle. Now you understand the picture a little.

I have shared enough information at this time.

Greetings, I AM Halisarius, Pleiadian Chief Commander, Historian and Teacher.

A Komo Ha Halima

Greetings, I AM Halisarius,

Pleiadian Chief Commander & Chief Leader,

Great Leader of the Galactic Federation of Light Society.

Part 42: How control began and still exists today

A long time ago we were friends with you. It was at a time when pain and fear were present on your earth. You were in a state of confusion and did not know what had happened, or how it happened. We calmed your fears and gave you healings of energy and light.

We are healers and transmitters of light. We understand much about your energy body and the realms in which you live. We understand how you are built and how dense you became.

A long, long time ago, before the Greatest Battle of Consciousness, well before you discovered the lower dimensions of earth, you played with light. You could move from plane to plane with ease. Life was easy and fun. You did not know war, you did not know pain. You did not understand anger. You were perfect, discovering your own creator within you and your magnificence that you held.

That changed when control and fear entered the atmospheres in your area of play. You could not understand why these beings came and why they took over your lives. You could not understand what they wanted and why they were cruel.

Many people died in the battle against these tyrants. They took control of you like animals. They raped the women to have offspring and then killed the women who gave birth to their offspring. The women who gave birth to their offspring would not have survived the birth anyway because the babies were too large.

They made sure to numb you and put great fear into you. You were forced to be their slaves. They came with machinery to mine your earth and they were largely after your gold.

They created slaves of your race to mine their treasures to use it for fuel and for their planets at home.

They carried powerful weapons. Many of those weapons were controlled with their mind. These weapons could destroy large areas at a time and people feared these weapons.

Slowly, over time, you forgot who you were. You forgot you were from the stars and instead, you lived day to day and became denser and denser. You did not remember anything else but work. Your memories of joy disappeared and your original DNA that was perfect with light from the stars was reduced. They shrunk your DNA, they tested it and they made sure your coding was not of star light anymore. They desired control. They desired to make you their slaves.

There is much to teach you about these beings. However, we do not want to place more fear within you. Already, when many read these pages, fear will creep in.

Creating fear within you is not our intention as Pleiadians of Light. Our intention is to educate you and to help you become free from these dark beings.

You may ask, free from them? But we do not see them anymore? We are free now, are we not?

We ask you to look at your world for a moment. How are you free? You are numb. You do not remember your ancestry. You do not remember the planets you are truly from. You do not remember the love you truly are. You only remember pain and fear which has been imprinted into your cellular system for hundreds of thousands of years.

How are you free dear ones? Can you not see that you are a slave class, walking around day by day, wondering how you will survive the coming decades? Wondering who will set you free?

Many of you pray to God to set you free and to find your salvation. Surely then, you admit you are not free. How are you still slaves? Look at your system. You are not free. You work, you pay, you work and you pay. You are slaves to a worldwide system and surely your New World Order, that promised better systems in your life has not come to be, has it?

Please dear ones. Please, we urge you to wake up. They are here still controlling the majority of people.

Greetings, I AM Halisarius, your dear old friend. I was with you as a great teacher and a friend in many of your past lifetimes on other planets and in Lemuria.

A Komo Ha Halima

Greetings, I AM Halisarius,

Pleiadian Chief Commander & Chief Leader,

Great Leader of the Galactic Federation of Light Society.

Part 43: You have the keys to your restoration of consciousness

How happy we are that you are reading these pages. We, as Pleiadians are wondering, if we have expanded your mind? Have we given you food for thought? If already you are looking at your world differently, could these stories we tell you be true? Please look at your world again and again and study it and then feel free to go into your heart to answer that question.

We go a long time back, you and us Pleiadian Members of Light Society. We were able to guide you a long time ago and bring you instruction and gifts. You trusted us as we showed you how to move beyond much of your pain and gave you hope to restoring yourselves again.

You, as a race had opportunities in the past to restore your DNA and yourselves once again. We showed you the power within you and fought against these beings of darkness.

We (I refer not to only us as Pleiadians but many of our Star Brothers and Sisters from many Dimensions and Planetary Existences) battled against these beings who took over your planet to bring darkness and fear.

We fought in the skies and we fought many times on the ground of your earth. Many of our people also died in the wars. We are proud warriors and when the fight is right, we do not fear the fight for we know our rewards of deep spiritual growth is strong.

We believe when we die in a battle for light, we return to another lifetime with greater gifts gained. Upon returning to a new incarnation, because of our evolution and our great awareness, we remember much of our past lives, unlike you who are asleep and you need to be woken up.

You exist in a denser energy than us. Hence you forget. You forget for many reasons. One of the great reasons why you, our family and friends of light, desired to come back at this time of the fulfillment of the great prophecies, is you knew the time of greater awareness and awakening was upon you.

You desired to be a part of this awakening and you desired to play a part in taking confusion away from your planet.

You may not remember these contracts you made between yourselves in Spirit, but you together desire to bring restoration back to your plane.

You are all important in these plans of the Divine Will and we are working along with you to restore much of what has been forgotten. We as Pleiadians often call your earth, 'Paradise Forgotten.' You will be happy to know that your 'Paradise will Return,' upon your earth.

How will it be restored? Again, you must look inside of yourselves. You have the keys of restoration within you. We can guide you, as your Angels and Guides also can, but you can only access it yourselves. It is you who has the key and the answers to mankind's 'Restoration of Consciousness.'

These beings of rebellion who do not desire you to understand these keys within you, know also of the great prophecy and they will fight against light. They will do anything and everything they can to keep you fighting and in fear among yourselves.

Who are they now? You may wonder this. You cannot see them in the physical arena of your dimension. You can see however, their work. Their work is confusion and fear. Their work is of darkness. Their work is working against light.

Your world is divided, light against dark, dark against light. Some of you, dear friends, do not believe in the battle of the dark. Is there true dark? Is dark evil?

Many of you may believe in evil. Again, this is the work of the dark, to make darkness seem evil.

How much fear they have placed within you. You still believe this to this day, even though the churches have no longer a hold over you in the way they did only a few years ago. Look how much you have freed yourselves from the bondage of the churches in the last few decades. Your churches are finding it difficult to keep control over their people. They constantly invent new ways to keep the people interested.

Control and fear was to keep the people in a limited space. The way to control a human is using great mind control.

You may suggest that mind control is not part of your game; that you are not controlled and that you feel free.

Again, we wish to help you understand that you are controlled by your society.

Do you watch your television transmissions? Or perhaps work in your society? How much do you depend on your money system? How much do you depend on understanding the people and what they fear? How much do you fear in your life?

What is freedom? Freedom is freedom from your illusion of fear. Understand all that you believe in is an illusion and that fear does not have energy at all when it is given the opportunity to be starved. People feed the energy of fear by believing in it.

A Komo Ha Halima

Greetings, I AM Halisarius,

Pleiadian Chief Commander & Chief Leader,

Great Leader of the Galactic Federation of Light Society.

Part 44: Darkness will surrender to the Great Light

Greetings, and our warmest welcome to all our readers. I am your faithful Guide through these pages. I AM Halisarius your faithful friend, one who visited your plane many times, along with other star brothers and sisters, together with my own star brothers and sisters, from the Pleiadian Realms of Existence.

We, as Pleiadians are fond of our brothers and sisters on earth. We discuss you much and our children know of you as well. We talk about your past and about the great warships coming from the skies to take over your planet.

They ask us many questions. 'How does the story end? Tell us?'

Like your children on earth, our children are curious and keen with desire to understand.

How will your story end? You can only answer that, our dear friends.

Here I would like to discuss a little what we have done for you and what we will do for you in the near future.

Please understand we cannot take charge of your lessons or your pain. You must find the keys yourself and unravel your mysteries of your history. You must understand the power within you and work with your energies to create a power within them to help you understand your love and to feel the love and the greatness between all.

You must learn to connect once again with your true power within you.

We, Pleiadians, are time jumpers. We have much technology. Your scientists would be greatly interested in our technology and how far we have come. We desire to share it with you one day, when you are ready and you are able to work with it without greed and without your anger.

If you were to see our technology now, if you were to have it now, you would turn it against your own people and destroy many, like you have done in the past.

In the past, we gave you many of our gifts and some of you turned against your own people and destroyed cities and many people. We do not desire for you to do this again. We will wait until your hearts change.

I will discuss some of what we have done for you in the past in further pages.

As you know we like to tell stories to help you become more awakened within you. Do you feel your mind expanding as we tell you these stories?

We are transmitting rays of light within your light bodies to help you remember who you are. It is important that you understand the greatness within you.

If we were to tell you that your very lives depend on it, we wonder how you would take this comment.

Again, it is not to put more fear into you, but it is to help you grow beyond your energies and bands of fear. Understand that you are important to us, and to all the universe, and we desire to bring you to your awareness of your greatness and of your keys within you to help you remember all that you are.

Your fear and anger is not who you are. The Family of Light within the energy coding of light does not work with anger and fear. These energies only came into your DNA, and into the very depths within you, when you were exposed to fear.

Again, to understand light more, one must be exposed to fear and darkness. How can you feel and understand light when you do not understand dark?

Here I will answer my question that I raised before. Is dark evil? In the universal energies of all that is, in the cosmic laws of energies, the answer is no. There is no true evil. Evil does not exist, for all is made of light. When energy is made from light it cannot turn into true evil.

However, darkness within light; the shadow of light, is unevolved light. Dark shadows must come to the surface to be healed and for light to become stronger. Shadows of light then become mature and healed.

You have the opportunity on this planet earth to rid all energies that have held you back for hundreds of thousands of years, to become healed. When you force this healing to happen, these energies that are unhealed and are standing in the shadows of light are then forced to surrender to light and they must then surrender themselves to light.

This is a prophecy which must come true.

'In those days,' so it is recorded in the Book of Holiness, 'Darkness will surrender to the Great Light. The Universal Light will become His once again and peace throughout the Universal Bodies of Light will be restored.

'The Sovereign One will say, 'Look, all I have created is good and is in balance. Let us enjoy light and let us feast in light, for the day of salvation has come.''

Greetings, I AM Halisarius, Pleiadian Chief Commander and your Teacher.

We are your Guardians

We are your Guardians,

of your Planet Earth.

We have been assigned,

to take care of you,

to allow you to grow,

without self-destruction,

to help you experience,

your greater love coming,

to allow you to understand,

who you truly are.

We gave you the time,

to discover your greater love.

It is love that will bring you,

into your greater knowledge,

into your greater power,

of the greater love.

You are here to discover

your greater gifts within you.

A Komo Ha Halima

Greetings, I AM Halisarius,

Pleiadian Chief Commander & Chief Leader,

Great Leader of the Galactic Federation of Light Society.

Part 45: We are Guardians of Planet Earth

We have technology to jump time. We have machinery to help us go to a time that is exact. It can be in your future or past.

We can still travel to your past. This is how we were able to intercept to help you on your journey in your past to create greater pathways for your future.

We have travelled to the future and placed several seeds of outcomes in place. With our guidance and steering we were able to help you awaken. We placed different scenarios in place and we were able to calculate how your journey would be. This is how we have been able to guide you to the greatest scenarios possible.

We have been able to plant seeds of light in the right places and based on their possible outcome we were able to calculate your outcome.

We cannot calculate exactly what will happen. We are not permitted to interfere with your evolution.

However, we can create different outcomes to help you survive. We have stepped in several times in your history to change the outcome because your path would have been fatal. We have stopped nuclear explosions and we have stopped a nuclear war.

We are Guardians of the Earth.

This may surprise you. Guardians of the earth? Yes. You certainly need them.

Why is it necessary for you to have Guardians? It is because you hold keys not only to your evolution of your planet but to the rest of the Universal Planetary Bodies of Existence.

Does that surprise you? Many of you debate existence of life on other planets. Why then, do you not know more of our existence if this is the case, you may ask?

This is because it is not the time yet for us to come to you. You are to discover more about yourselves before you receive us on your doorstep. At this moment in your history, it would not be safe for us to come to you. You would take us prisoner and experiment greatly on us, like I have mentioned in previous pages.

We will investigate together with you, why your existence at this time is crucial as beings on your plane and how you affect others on other planetary realms of existence.

You are in the center of a theatrical play. You are in the center of a battle, a battle between light and dark.

Greetings, I AM Halisarius, Pleiadian Leader. I bring Star Nations together to evolve into love.

Your greater soul journey

Your greater soul journey,

is to discover love,

to discover greatness,

to discover expansion,

in each lifetime you travel.

For what is love?

What is greatness?

What is expansion?

That is your greatest mission.

Each time you discover more,

you bring more light into yourself.

Your light brings more light to the earth,

because of your love for your earth,

which to you is very precious,

as planet earth,

is part of your soul journey,

and it too wants to expand,

along with you.

A Komo Ha Halima

Greetings, I AM Halisarius,
Pleiadian Chief Commander & Chief Leader,
Great Leader of the Galactic Federation of Light Society.

Part 46: Your greater journey

I have returned. How wonderful it is that we can share with you our stories. Do you understand them? There is much to learn and think upon.

All through your history you have learned much. You have explored much. You explored times of peace and times of war.

You found that you had much strength because of war times. You found your survival skills. You found your fear could leave you behind and as a result go into total disconnection.

Many of you still carry disconnection and numbness in this life. Have you considered where it comes from?

Many of you do not want to go into your feelings. Many of you are confused with your anger issues. Why did they come? Can you not see that it is linked to your past incarnations?

Have you truly had past incarnations?

We desire to touch upon these matters as these matters are about exploring you.

You live many lives. At times you have lives together. You may be living one life and another at the same time. You often call this, 'Parallel lives of existence.'

Why would you live different lives and parallel lives? What is the greater purpose of this?

Here I would like to give you a lesson about where you come from and why you incarnate here to this plane.

Many of you also incarnate on many other planets, not only on this earth. Many of you are star travelers. Does this surprise you? Again we are mentioning other life on other planets. How does this affect you? Do you feel comfortable with the idea? Perhaps intrigued? Perhaps warm? Perhaps confused because you do not believe in other beings?

When you look up at the stars you see only a minute portion of your universe. In our eyes, your Milky Way is as small as the tip of a needle. We know much about the planetary existences and yet we also know very little.

Can you begin to understand the vastness of the universe out there? Can you imagine how many beings could exist? If you feel it is difficult to believe and imagine, can you begin to open your mind to the possibility of other beings existing on other planetary existences?

You may be wondering, if you incarnate time and time again, why? What would be the reason?

Understand our friends, that life is not all what it seems on your planet and that all of creation is about evolution and moving on into greater energies of love. It is always about discovering and progressing forwards.

We, all as One Great Brotherhood of all races, can unite together and come in peace together, living in harmony with each other, living the Great Cosmic Laws of the Great Universe, to create harmony with each other and to understand truly the great love for each other.

How do you evolve into this greater understanding? Could it be done when you only have one life?

Look at the life you have. It is short. You may consider your life to be long. Yet, look at the trees which are standing tall above you. Many of them are far older than you. Why would they become older and yet you with an intelligent brain only live for a short lifetime?

Does this make sense to you if this life was all there is?

Like I have mentioned before, we as Pleiadians; those of us who are highly evolved, are greatly aware of our past lives. We remember the reasons of our past lives and we are not asleep and numb to our past lives and the greater purpose of our journey.

You also have a journey. 'The Great Journey of Your Soul.' This is what we call it. Your Soul knows all about you. How beautiful it shines in the light. You are that light. You grow in the light of your Soul when you gain a higher awareness of all that is.

We too have greater souls. We are guided by our greater souls and we connect deeply with our soul. Our young ones are taught to expand in the light of their soul also and when we allow ourselves to do so, our intelligence and love soars. Hence, our evolution is quick. We all live in the same purpose and some of us, who are still young, are taught how to sit in the power and the light of their Soul Light.

We are their teachers and guides, as we are yours.

Your greater journey is about finding love and expansion. It is about connecting you with who you are and connecting you to your Source of Love and Light.

Greetings, I AM Halisarius, Pleiaidan Leader and Guide.

A Komo Ha Halima

Greetings, I AM Halisarius,
Pleiadian Chief Commander & Chief Leader,
Great Leader of the Galactic Federation of Light Society.

Part 47: The defiance of the dark

Why am I here? Because it is the time for you to come out of your pain and into greater understanding that you can become free.

How grand it is to have this time. We, as a people of the Pleiadian Realms, have looked forward to this time.

Many have been frightened of this part on your time line. Many in the past prophesied the end of times around 2012 and many of you became frightened, praying it would not be your end.

2012 was a special time for you as you played in the cosmic party of all times deeper. Fireworks went off on our realms as you came into greater portals of light and higher frequencies of understanding and awakening. The time of the Great Awakening was here. We celebrated the heralding in of greater consciousness.

We celebrated this and held our own meditations on our planetary system. We had many prayers and visions for mankind's awakening and coming together.

Guidance from Archangels and Divine Masters were given to us. Times were given to us so that we could help you in greater ways.

We, as Pleiadians, have always been a part of your acceleration. We have always been part of your guidance system and a part of your teaching instruction.

Many thousands of years ago, vast numbers of you, (after the fall of light and into the ages of great darkness) were frightened. It seemed as if you had lost your memories, and you had.

Your DNA was disorganized, your bodies became more fragile, you did not live as long and you had deep fears imprinted within you.

Many we worked with we helped escape to other countries to help you become free from your leaders of darkness.

Many of those we worked with were never captured and stayed more pure. However, fear still crept in and over the many, many years, because of mating with those of the disrupted DNA, the people with purer DNA were also infected. This infection was like a disease.

However, these ones who stayed purer kept their DNA stronger and were able to keep light alive and in a great way, give healing to the ones who were hurt the greatest.

Hence, there were different groups of people on your planet. There were groups who had been captured and were deeply enslaved by these beings not of light and groups who escaped enslavement. These were able to keep light alive when the beings tried to destroy light.

These different groups included civilizations from the stars that came to your planet. They came to preserve your light History. They were determined for light not be exterminated.

Some of the enslaved were able to escape and find these groups also. We welcomed them and kept them safe.

These beings of darkness were not able to access all areas of earth as we, (many star beings of light) defined perimeters, (grids of energies around sacred portals) so that light, no matter how much they pushed anger and fear into the planet, would never totally be eradicated.

However, the choice to remember the Great Light in the times of the Great Awakening would always be yours to have. Would you be strong enough to access greater frequencies and find it again to open higher dimensions of light within you?

These were questions waiting to be answered. Ancient civilizations such as the Mayans were 'Guardians of Light.' They guarded the gateway of light and had access to great portals of time, existence, parallel universes. They knew what 'reality' was and were not caught in the 'illusion.'

Here I would like to describe these beings of darkness closer and I will allow you to understand them better.

I will be telling my stories once again. Stories are a good way to expand your mind.

Many tens of millions of years ago, (and I speak broadly) many races existed in the light. Like all brothers and sisters, they interacted with one planetary system after another, sharing their resources, sharing their knowledge and wisdom.

Many of them lived peacefully. Many of them attended to the universal rules set in place to create unity, evolution, peace and greatness.

However, like in all stories, there were the goodies and the baddies. You may have heard names such as the Reptilians. I do not desire to share with you exact details at this stage of how many there are.

Why? Because if you knew how many there truly are and what they could truly do to you, it would put you into a state of panic and fear.

We are your friends and we do not desire to do this to you. We desire to make you aware but not create fear.

On your planet there are good ones and not so good ones. Please understand that it is no different on many of these planets. We cannot consider them evil but consider them as not working in light and not yet evolved in light and as yet needing to learn the ways of light. Many of them have forgotten how to love and what love is.

A long, long time ago in our history of the universe, these cold beings decided that in order to evolve and grow more quickly, they would need to find out about their own weapons and strength.

They did not desire peace anymore. They came together as a party and decided to go against the Universal Laws. They decided to create havoc.

They created havoc on many planets. They took planets as if they were their own. They took beings in peace with each other, into slavery and bondage and created slave classes and fear.

They were after power and control. They believed that power and control was their key to evolution; the fast lane.

Many battles followed on many planetary systems. We, as Pleiadians, also were involved in many battles trying to keep these dark ones away from our star brothers and sisters.

These beings of defiance, gathered masses upon masses of beings on their side, making them believe they could take over the universe. They convinced others with their sly ways and twisted understandings that the 'old cosmic laws' did no longer apply in their 'modern' time. They created their own laws. They created their own ways of controlling. They created their own government and own rules. On their own planets, the ones who dwelled in peace were forced to follow their rules. If they refused they would face severe punishment.

Their energies became more and more controlling. Their hate and anger grew among each other. They fought for place of leadership.

They found much in their ways of research. They found by creating time tunnels or portals as you would call them, they could place these tunnels onto a planet of their choosing and create a sort of vacuum to gather up energies of pain and fear and portal it through to their own planet. These methods enhanced their own energies as their energy source was, and is to this day, pain and anger.

Can you understand how they have used your people to feed themselves? They do not feed on physical food like you do. They live in a different dimension and feed on energy. These beings feed on your pain and fear. The greater the pain and fear you have, the greater the power they have over you.

As you can imagine, we as a Planetary Cosmic System were not happy. We needed to put systems in place and fast to resolve this crucial universal issue.

What were these systems? What did the Universe do in this case? We will return soon.

Greetings, I AM Halisarius, Pleiadian Leader. In the Galactic Federations of Light Society I am part of a Great Team ensuring the Cosmic Laws of Light are upheld.

A Komo Ha Halima

Greetings, I AM Halisarius,

Pleiadian Chief Commander & Chief Leader,

Great Leader of the Galactic Federation of Light Society.

Part 48: Higher organizations in the Great Universe

We wonder how you are finding these pages? Are they exciting for you? Are they making sense to you? Do you feel truth within these pages? Are you remembering these battles?

Many of you are. You are awakening to the whispers within you. These are stirrings within.

The Great Universe is organized into different organizations. They are large and they are vast. All organizations in greatness and light are in harmony with each other and we work together with Cosmic Laws of the Great Universal Light. We come to agreements based on the Great Laws and seek to find answers based on the Great Laws of the Cosmic Universe.

In this lesson, I would like to introduce you to these higher organizations. I would like to introduce you to them to help you appreciate them.

Here, we are keeping our stories simple. In our reality, they are far more complicated and far more in detail than I will explain it in these few words. The detail at this time in your history, you do not need to know. There is no use in knowing the details. It would not help you spiritually move forward and give you answers you are seeking.

The way the universe is organized is complex.

The universe is organized in such a way to allow all to grow together.

First, I would like to illustrate how we run our government and then we will move on to the grander governments.

We, as Pleiadians, also have a government on our planet like you do. However, ours is run with harmony and love, for love is the basis of our lives.

When we come into the Great Organization of our people, we have travelled these same paths for lifetimes. We have been trained and we train other evolved Pleiadians to follow our steps.

We have harmony together and have grown beyond disruptions of pain and anger. We are constantly surrounded in energies of infusion of everlasting love.

You would be wise to learn from us also. Look at how you choose your leaders. How much do they dwell in love and higher knowledge? How great is their desire to lead people into greater dimensions of love?

For you are in a great dimensional shift. Your pain will intensify and your love will also. Where will your choice be?

Many spiritual seekers on your plane understand the term, 'The Great Sacred White Brotherhood.' Who are they and what is their role?

There are many Elders who belong to the, 'Great Sacred White Brotherhood,' not only twelve or twenty-four Elders, but many, many more.

Each of these Elders has a significant role to play in the Universal Scheme of Laws. They are all there for one reason only. To unite the Universe and the Sanctification of the Holy Sovereignty to bring everything to perfection and unity so that, 'The One,' can expand into, 'Greater Love.'

Among this Great Sacred White Brotherhood, there is no disharmony. This council exists in greater dimensions.

Their role is to create laws. These laws are called Great Cosmic Laws. These Great Cosmic Laws keep everything in order.

Many books on higher dimensions are written by the Sacred White Council. Each universe has keepers or guardians to look after certain parts of the universe. Every universe is created for a specific reason.

Here, I would like to point out, please understand that there is no accident to any of creation. There is no sudden 'Big Bang,' for nothing as many of you believe. There is a divine purpose for everything and everything is tightly structured and planned.

There are also other foundations or organizations that have been placed to look after a particular body of planets. There are many of these. We belong to The Galactic Federation of Light Society.

They organize part of our universe. The leaders of the planetary systems that belong to the federation come together with each other to advance, create plans together and share technology and information. We discuss how we feel about situations and we keep in touch with each other.

How does this fit in with my story? You will find out soon.

Greetings, I AM Halisarius, Pleiadian Leader. I am a great fighter for Love and Light. My fight has always been to unify the Great Star Realms to allow all to grow and evolve to strong love within.

A Komo Ha Halima

Greetings, I AM Halisarius,
Pleiadian Chief Commander & Chief Leader,
Great Leader of the Galactic Federation of Light Society.

Part 49: Your fear is a virus

We are here holding a space for you at this moment for you to heal in higher places. We are placing a frequency within you to heal your spiritual heart. Many of your hearts have been shut down because of the mistrust on your planet.

How can you trust one another? The love between your people has been lost. The trust between your people has been lost. The fear has become great.

Your fear around you is like a virus. A virus changes does it not? It constantly takes on new and greater forms to fight against healing. It changes to find a way to survive. Hence, you are having much trouble in the medical profession because the virus is alive. The virus is an entity within itself and it will fight to keep alive.

What will kill viruses? What feeds viruses? That you have not discovered yet.

Does something feed a virus? Yes it does. A virus on your planet came because of fear. When fear is locked in a cell it creates a weakness within the cell and allows itself to be a breeding ground.

When you begin to understand how energetically you are able to become stronger and eliminate fear on your planet, you will rid many of your diseases.

Sickness eats you because of the fear you hold. You were not supposed to understand sickness, although it was a great probability you would experience great disturbances and fluctuations within your energy body of light, leading to disruptions within your physical body.

Hence, it is important to understand yourself and how grand you are. It is important to begin to appreciate who you are, to fight off and eradicate all that seems to harm you.

Remembering that everything around you is a reflection of what it is that you hold on the inside and that you are living in an illusion that constantly reflects back to you what you are holding within you, until it is recognized and released.

You may consider this deeper. How can you live in an illusion of pain and how does your reflection reflect back to you like a mirror?

This is a lesson in itself. Please let me explain the beauty of your lessons.

We as Pleiadians in our realms of existence learned this long ago and hence because of our understanding, we climbed out of our pain and into higher energies because we understood energy flow and how to work with it and not against it. Please understand however, when I mention 'pain' it does not refer to your state of pain.

A Komo Ha Halima, Greetings, I AM Halisarius, Pleiadian Leader and Great Leader of the Galactic Federation of Light Society. I organize large teams to do the great work for your people to bring them back to love consciousness.

A Komo Ha Halima

Greetings, I AM Halisarius,

Pleiadian Chief Commander & Chief Leader,

Great Leader of the Galactic Federation of Light Society.

Part 50: Learning to play with Energies of Love

Your energies on your plane are heavy when you do not understand how to work with the energies.

At this moment in time, you are able to climb out of the painful energies into the higher energies of love. These energies feel more of 'love' and 'light' to work in and are more joyful. In these energies you will receive the love that you have been looking for. For you are already able to exist within those energies.

It is like you are living on top of a mountain. A beautiful mountain has fresh air. You can breathe without feeling the heaviness of life. Perhaps down below there is a valley. In the valley many people are wondering about their life and are constantly complaining and becoming sick with energy sicknesses and heaviness. You, on the mountain however, are free from the disease and the sickness from the valley because you are not around them.

It is similar to your life. Many people are in the dark wanting answers. They cannot see the answers and so they carry on with their miserable life, complaining, hurting, blaming each other, being angry and crying the victim. They live in a vicious circle.

They may not see themselves being in this cycle of pain because being in the pain may seem ordinary to them. They do not understand how to be, other than being in the pain.

For those who understand spiritual values and understand illusions, they are able to climb out of this cycle of pain and be in the energies of joy and love instead.

Your 'realities'

Your 'realities,'
are based on your beliefs,
which are created,
in your mind.
Your 'realities,'
are an illusion,
reflecting back to you,
what you believe,
within your consciousness.
Learn to change what you believe,
learn to become strong and rise,
with your thoughts and ways,
and then your greater thoughts,
will change your 'reality,'
to reflect peace, love and wisdom,
the higher forms of 'reality,'
back to you.

A Komo Ha Halima

Greetings, I AM Halisarius,

Pleiadian Chief Commander & Chief Leader,

Great Leader of the Galactic Federation of Light Society.

Part 51: Your illusion of life

All things are an illusion around you. Even the mirror reflecting back to you in the morning is an illusion. You believe your face to be real because you have seen it often and you have made your reflection a reality. In reality you are not there. In reality you are an energy believing yourself to be real and solid.

Your mind is powerful and it is purposely made this way. It is made this way so you can experience your life. How else can you learn and grow on this earth plane? How else can you live your greater journey of life?

The information I will give to you now may be a little difficult for some of you to comprehend, so please read it and re-read it if you have difficulty.

All of life is an illusion and all of life is a part of you that is on a path to help you grow. Nothing is as real as you think it is and everything surrounding you is a part of your cycle. You are alone in this world of illusion and when you understand this, you understand the concept more of 'The Oneness', because you are part of the Oneness and the Oneness is a part of you.

Again I say this may be difficult for you to comprehend and understand. Why? Because you believe you are truly here and yet you are not. You are not here on the earth plane at all. You are an illusion of another part that dwells in the realms of light. You are a part of the greater self that desires to learn how to climb out of pain and into love because it desires to understand greater love.

What does this mean in your 'reality' terms? Friends, if we told you there is no point in being angry or upset at anyone else because when you are angry with someone else, you are seeing the reflection of yourself. How will you 'reflect' back upon this thought?

You are hurting in some part of you when you are angry. You are not letting go and loving yourself as much as you could.

Therefore, it is important to be forgiving and to allow the parts you are angry with to let go and let it be gone. Do not be angry but grow in the love.

When people understand this incredible truth on your planet, you can move forward. It is love that is the key to all your greatness and your healing.

Returning back to my previous lesson about the virus, the virus will keep growing until you learn to love and forgive. You will find that you will become stronger and your sicknesses will have no hold over you anymore.

Also when love is strongly on your plane, your plane will become free from fear and anger as energies of fear and anger will not be able to survive. Then, these beings of great defiance will no longer be able to feed off you anymore. The lack of fear and anger on your plane will starve them and fear and anger energies on your plane will disappear more and more. Hence they will have no control over you anymore.

Your mind is incredibly important. You control your energy with your mind. You control your direction with your mind.

We ask you then, are you ready to learn about your higher reality of living?

We will return in a few moments. Greetings, I AM Halisarius, Chief Leader on the Pleiadian Realms of Light.

A Komo Ha Halima

Greetings, I AM Halisarius,
Pleiadian Chief Commander & Chief Leader,
Great Leader of the Galactic Federation of Light Society.

Part 52: The power of fear

You have learned much in these pages already. There are more lessons to follow. In the previous lessons you learned more about fear energies and reality energies and how you are living in pools of illusions of energies of fear.

Fear creates challenges on your planet. Fear in itself is a virus that is contagious. Fear travels fast and greatly. Fear is felt instantly on the other side of your planet. Fear is destructive and powerful.

Do you realize the power of your fear?

As you have already learned, the beings of darkness that came to enslave you, created fear within your consciousness.

Before their arrival you had no concept of fear. Fear was not in your vocabulary. You only knew power within yourself. You could time travel, travel with us, travel to other dimensions, create together, dwell together in true love, greatness and harmony.

You did not have sickness and you did not age.

Does that sound like paradise? It was. Everything was 'perfect and good,' in the eyes of your 'Creators' who created you in love and greatness.

Your Creators, have created many other planets and beings and they are good Beings of Love. They are intelligent and work with great love force for their creation. They have the power to create and change energies. They are skilled at changing multidimensional layers of energy frequencies to create beauty. They understand greater purpose and work in alignment with the Greater Force, the One, the Source and the Light.

When these dark beings came to your earth, they desired to control you and place the greatest fear within you that they could.

They succeeded well. We will return to their purpose more in the coming pages.

First, let us look at fear and tell you in our stories how destructive it was to your nature.

You were a perfect, aligned race. This perfect race knew about other civilizations. It knew about their visitors and had complete trust. Other star beings from other universes shared with you their technology and their greatness. You knew much. You knew how to build houses and create love. You knew more than you could imagine at this time.

You lived in peace. You dwelled in unity. You were great inventors as well.

Suddenly these dark beings came from out of space. They raped your women, took the men and created their own species in their own laboratories.

Does that sound strange to you? Does it sound strange that these beings had their own laboratories on their ships?

Please understand the intelligence they have. They are far more intelligent than you are at this present moment.

They desired to have a slave class of people who stayed 'ignorant' to their own consciousness. They knew who you were and they knew of the great secrets in the universe. They knew why you were created here and did not want you to find your secret, because if you knew, you could stand up against them.

What are we talking about? What are these secrets?

Please understand that these records within these books of Earth have stayed secret until times of the 'Great Awakening.' Not even our own people were able to give you this information until this time because of Divine Timing.

It has been safely kept until the right time.

What time is this? It is when you must discover the greatest secret of yourselves.

Why? Because if you stay in the illusion that your reality is all there is, these dark beings of great defiance will create greater darkness on your planet because you will allow it to happen.

We know that will not happen. We have faith in you. We have seen your outcome. However, the outcome also depends on you. After all, you live in a time of freedom and this privilege of living in freedom is yours to have. This has much to do with your purpose and the Divine Secret of all times.

What secret? How are you involved?

Please read on. You will discover this in the coming few pages.

Greetings, I AM Halisarius, Pleiadian Leader, Pleiadian Teacher. We as Pleiadians of Love have great love for you.

A Komo Ha Halima

Greetings, I AM Halisarius,

Pleiadian Chief Commander & Chief Leader,

Great Leader of the Galactic Federation of Light Society.

Part 53: The time is here to step out of your fear

We desire you to understand these lessons. We hope they give you greater information and that they are stretching your imagination and your thinking.

When you imagine, your brain cells grow. Do you realize this? Your brain keeps growing. It keeps repairing. It is a magnificent organ and it is well preserved. The brain does not age if it is used well. It can reverse aging and disease. Its cells work faster than you realize and you are able to heal your brain faster than you realize.

How?

With your thought and imagination.

Often, when a person is sick or has had an injury, they will go into a place of great despair. You are not healing if you are in these spaces. Please understand the power of your body and your mind. When you discover the strength within you, you can get out of your wheelchairs and heal from your diseases.

You are living an illusion. Which illusion do you desire to live in? Heal your viewpoints and then you will begin to heal also. Suffer with yourself and your reality will reflect this also.

Are we being hard on you here friends? We are not. We have the greatest love for you. We desire to help you understand the power within you and help you to understand that all is an illusion, including your wrinkles as you age and your grey hair. You receive those because you believe in your reality and believe in aging.

In reality you do not truly exist on this planet at all. It is an illusion of the mind.

We desire to take you back to the time when the laboratories were in place. Why? Is it to bring you into fear?

No friends, it is to take you out of fear and into understanding. Again I will pose the question; why is this important at this time? Because you are living in a time of Awakening and the secrets of the past are unfolding.

Many of your leaders will not want you to read this book. However, our energies will not allow them to stop these books. Why not? Because it is the time the power is given back to the people. It is the time when you begin to awaken to all that you are. It is the time to stop these beings once and for all and to take charge of your own power because your power is precious.

You are included in this war and we, as your Pleiadian friends, are also involved as well as all Beings in this universe and many other universal galactic dimensions.

A Komo Ha Halima, Greetings beloved friends, I AM Halisarius, Pleiadian Chief Leader and Chief Advisor on the Galactic Federation of Light.

A Komo Ha Halima

Greetings, I AM Halisarius,
Pleiadian Chief Commander & Chief Leader,
Great Leader of the Galactic Federation of Light Society.

Part 54: What happened to your original DNA?

A Komo Ha Halima, I AM Halisarius, and we come in peace and love for all people of the human race. We desire to teach you how to live in greatness, to bring love and peace back onto your plane, and for you to live in your greatness.

First of all, let me take you back to the time when these beings of darkness were here on this earth and let me explain what they did to you.

We have already explained what they did to the people. Let us go into the laboratories where they restructured your original DNA patterns.

It was a grim time. It was a time not to be proud of. You can imagine what they did. They dissected the human and studied its DNA and discovered how to rid your consciousness and awareness and create a species that would simply follow their instructions under their control.

They had no time for working the mines themselves. They desired to have slaves to do all the work for them. They created their own species. They were you. This is where you come into the story.

You were the same as the light people before you, except now you were slowly being created in a painful denser version. The memories of who you were slowly disappeared. Your DNA shrunk. Their mind control is deep and heavy. They still have their power over you without you realizing it, because it is placed within your DNA to be controlled by them.

However, they did not realize that you would grow to a higher consciousness. Your DNA began to repair over time with light from the higher heavens and from star beings who cared for you very much. The light grids began to be formed with greater strength and many love energies returned to your planet.

Within your DNA there is a code that has always remained untouched that responds to higher frequencies of love. When higher frequency sounds are sounded in the universe, your awakening within occurs.

These beings of great defiance did not count on you remembering what love was about. They forgot about the most vital ingredient you were created with. Love. Love awakens you. Love heals you. Love is healing your DNA faster than you are realizing and because their dense cobweb net is disappearing quickly and is almost nil at this moment, masses are awakening to love energies.

For a moment here I will pause and allow you to consider all we have discussed. This information may be a little heavy for you at this moment. Countless questions may come to your mind. Or on the contrary, countless answers may have been answered.

What then happened to the evidence of the Light People who were your ancestors from the stars? We will discover this together in our next story.

Greetings, I AM Halisarius. I can be your friend and guide.

Confusion and fear

Confusion and fear,

are not of light,

but of dark.

It restricts your growth.

Restriction creates confusion.

Fear and suffering,

are within the planes,

of disharmony and pain,

the lower realms of denseness.

Choose to focus on the light,

for then the darkness will shift.

It will no longer have its power,

its hold over you,

and you will climb up higher,

into the love dimension,

where you will find your freedom,

love and peace.

A Komo Ha Halima

Greetings, I AM Halisarius,

Pleiadian Chief Commander & Chief Leader,

Great Leader of the Galactic Federation of Light Society.

Part 55: Your ancestors, light beings from the stars

By now you must have gathered how we love to tell stories. These stories have been kept in secret records. There have been records kept by many of our people and some have stayed secret until 'The Times of the End.'

What is so important that has been kept secret for so long? What is so important that you need to know about?

Again, you will find out soon.

In the last chapter I brought up the thought of what happened to the evidence of the Light People, your ancestors. If you are finding it difficult to comprehend and believe, I ask you why you are finding it difficult to understand. Could it not be possible that this all happened?

Please understand, as we have already stated that these beings of defiance are intelligent. They are not in light but they are not evil. There is no true evil in the universe. Their hearts became selfish and dark. Their purpose from being in the light turned to become greedy with power. They tasted power and it tasted good to them. They began to take what was not theirs to have. They forgot about love. Their hearts became cold, and distant from light.

Upon receiving the taste of taking what was not theirs to have, their greed became greater. They also carry fear. Their greatest fear is losing power. When they lose their power, they will have to surrender to light. This was the agreement. The Sacred White Brotherhood of Light views contracts such as this very seriously.

Please understand that much evidence of your ancestors has been lost on purpose. They did not want you to know of your past. They wanted to keep you in confusion. They have succeeded in the confusion. What does confusion lead to? It leads to disharmony, distrust, fear, anger, arguments, wars and killings.

You understand that most of your wars are based upon the arguments between the beliefs of your people? Do you truly think this was an accident? Was it? Or was it already decided many, many tens of thousands of years ago to bring destruction upon your plane in this fashion.

Is it possible that major wars and much trouble was planned a long time ago to bring you into their control by means of keeping you in separation, confusion and fear?

Greetings, I AM Halisarius, Pleiadian Chief Leader and your Teacher and Guide.

A Komo Ha Halima

Greetings, I AM Halisarius,

Pleiadian Chief Commander & Chief Leader,

Great Leader of the Galactic Federation of Light Society.

Part 56: The evidence; where is it?

Where is the evidence of your ancient history? Some of the evidence is right under your noses. You are living evidence of it. Your earth also has evidence to be uncovered when you are ready. Much of it sank into the oceans and most of it was destroyed many thousands of years ago.

These beings of great defiance did not want you to uncover your true history. It would give you answers. It would make you stronger. Imagine friends, if you turned your television on and a scientist had a report to say that proof of a person in your ancient history had been found with its perfect DNA intact. Imagine if you found proof of evidence that your ancestors were very powerful beings.

How would this change you? How would this create a greater awakening within you?

How did they destroy most of the evidence? They burned the bodies instead of burying them. They burned them well.

They also created a flood on your planet to wipe out much of the evidence they left behind with their laboratories and experiments. This was said to be done by God. It had nothing to do with the One who created all, for Divine Source is of great love.

Many stories that you believe in were given to you to make you frightened. Your fear is what they feed on. They are like vultures. They feed on the spiritually asleep people with deadened hearts.

Please do not take offence to this our friends. We do not see you this way. They however do.

Spiritually, the majority of people are not living with life in their hearts. You, as a race will be resurrected to light. You are awakening but they cannot feed off the living. Light they hate. They hate your love. They despise your awakening. They feed off the spiritually dead. Why? This is because they feed on your dense fear energies.

Vultures they are. Filth they are.

Are they still with you? Is their energy still leading you? Many of you have researched the answers well.

Yes, they do. They have your leaders under their control. Many of your leaders are controlled by this energy that is from them.

Most of them realize it and many of them celebrate these 'gods' to remind themselves of the importance of standing in alliance with these 'beasts' that call themselves 'your gods'.

Hence, you are in the greatest battle in history. At this time you do not comprehend it yet. You are receiving bits and pieces of information and you are fitting the puzzle together slowly. It is important to understand it slowly, for this information is about awakening you and understanding what your planet is doing to you energetically. You are in a Time of Awakening.

Do you have the courage to look within it more?

Greetings I AM Halisarius, Pleiadian Leader. I hold a great deal of power. I am an ancient teacher with much wisdom and love for all of life.

A Komo Ha Halima

Greetings, I AM Halisarius,

Pleiadian Chief Commander & Chief Leader,

Great Leader of the Galactic Federation of Light Society.

Part 57: Your ancient history in the times of Ancient Lemuria and Atlantis

We are going away from the subject of these dark beings of great defiance now, into another time period. Why? To help you remember more about who you are and more about your history.

It is important for you to understand the games of your history and to understand you.

Before the 'Great Fall of Consciousness,' when the people were peaceful and in love with all of life, life was good. Life was very good. We used to visit you often. We came to you and instructed you.

Although the Middle East was important for much of your beginning, there were other people in other places. Some of these histories go far back.

Many also after the invasion, fled and gathered into their own colonies and lived in other places, determined not to allow fear to come into their minds. They fought hard. They did well.

There were some of these sacred sites that these beings of great defiance and disloyal to the light were not allowed to enter because of your sacred spirituality.

We, as your Star Brothers and Sisters, helped you to set up energetic boundaries to keep them out. This was so that light would have a chance to grow on your earth before the almost complete time of darkness. This will be discussed a little further on.

We protected these sacred spaces. We dwelled with you in harmony and taught you how to succeed and live and most of all how to forgive. Many found it difficult to go into the forgiving places. They knew the pains many of their brothers and sisters had suffered. The light tried several times to send light people to the earth spaces. Many were destroyed by the ones not in the light. We set up a space to protect the light people to allow them to grow into great strength.

There were spiritual lands, where you lived lifetime after lifetime, desiring to bring light back to the earth and to have the original DNA patterning restored. This is how beloved your earth was to you.

One of these sacred lands (and there were more) protected from many energies of dark defiance, was Lemuria. This ancient land was protected by many star beings. We even gave you much technology to fight these beings of darkness off should they try to invade at that time.

The darkness never truly tried to intrude. It was impossible as your laser technology was incredibly advanced. We had protective shields set up to protect the light. Your memories were good although you were infected with pain at the beginning of this 'new' existence. You kept light awake on your planet.

Many of you protected your history by engraving your memories and who you truly were into crystals you had brought with you from the stars. You mourned and wept and yet you also rejoiced because you worked with light.

Ancient Spiritual Lemuria (as well as other spiritual civilizations around this time) was a special place for you. It was happy for many thousands of years. Many of you lived there countless incarnations, not only because of peace, but because of the determination to keep light alive on your planet and rid the universe from all resistance to love energies.

You wrote records of the history of humanity and you engraved it into the earth. You also engraved it into the crystals, knowing of its vibrational energy and the power that you do not yet understand to the full today. You will in the future. You will become greatly familiar with the energies because you will remember and the crystals will open their memories to you, when the Divine Time is here.

Many mysteries surround this time. How sad you were when Beloved Ancient Lemuria sank. How deeply grieved you were.

You protected your beloved land from darker energies so that nothing could destroy light that was hidden in the depths of the earth for it would rise again when the time was ripe.

Did you sink it? Did you sink Ancient Lemuria to protect its secrets? Yes, you did, largely. Not entirely, but you decided together to sink it to protect the treasures and the holy secrets.

As the land sank deep into the oceans, some of you travelled back to the stars, some of you took your boats and travelled to other lands with spiritual civilizations.

Your protectors of all of the sacred secrets in your history; a special group anointed by light to guard the secrets of Beloved Ancient Spiritual Lemuria for all times, had their tongues removed so that they could not utter the sacred secrets of the past.

Why not? What was so secret that they could not release?

These are the secrets locked in the books until the time of the greater awareness. In case you are wondering, our Blue Star, my transmitter, Suzanna Maria Emmanuel, was one of these Ancient Guardians. Her tongue was ripped out to keep the sacred secrets hidden until the very end.

Hence, she has the honor for these secrets to be revealed through her.

What happened to Atlantis? Would you like a little insight to Atlantis?

How the people in the past mourned Atlantis. It was a place of beauty, like Lemuria, and a place of wisdom. The people were mostly good, though some chose to rebel against their leaders. They had many spiritual laws, and we, as Pleiadians also taught them many of our laws.

The leader of Atlantis was generally a good man. A great man. A great commander and chief. Atlantis was friendly to many other nations including Lemuria in the old times and other nations such as Egypt. Atlantis was small and young compared to many others but it rose fast in power.

We, Pleiadians in Light, shared much technology with Atlantis. Our gifts helped their civilization to excel quickly. We taught Atlantians, as well as Lemurians and other civilizations, how to work with the power of crystal grids. Many gifts we gave also to good hearted Egyptians.

However, some of the Atlantians were not in light, in particular one army commander. When his heart grew dark and greedy he desired more control and power.

We had given Atlantis a very special crystal. This crystal was large and it was to protect the nations against the other beings not of light. It also could power up cities and create much good.

The story did not end well however. The technology of Atlantis was advanced. Their armies had laser guns and powerful weapons. They were well protected in case of an invasion.

We will continue soon our dear friends.

Greetings, I AM Halisarius, Pleiadian Chief Leader and your Guide through these pages.

A Komo Ha Halima

Greetings, I AM Halisarius,

Pleiadian Chief Commander & Chief Leader,

Great Leader of the Galactic Federation of Light Society.

Part 58: Continuation of your history of Ancient Lemuria and Atlantis

We will continue on with the stories of the ancient Lemurian and Atlantean history.

As we continue the story of Ancient Lemuria and Atlantis, times were not smooth when greed and anger desired to be present in Atlantis.

Also, during those times, arguments broke out between the Elders of Atlantis and Lemuria. In particular, about evolving and giving positions to the 'Elite' class. The Elders in Ancient Lemuria lived within their hearts but Atlantis had other ideas since power and control was becoming their strong focus. Frustrations between the nations were growing.

The commander who grew greedy in Atlantis desired to rule more. He desired to have more and blackmailed his leader. Atlantis was blown up in a feud over ownership. Hence, the colossal explosion sunk Atlantis. Even now, this large crystal is still seen at times lying at the bottom of the ocean. It is magnetic with its power and although it still lies at the bottom of the ocean, it still holds magnificent power.

In reality, it was more complicated than what we have told you. However, we have explained their history in as few words to help you understand briefly about what happened in your history.

We also left planet earth. We were sad. Our gifts; our technology had been misused and caused much destruction. We felt truly sorry for the knowledge we had given you.

This is why we will not share with you our technology until you have reached a time of greater unity between yourselves.

Please understand these lessons our dear friends. We made sure our technology we gave you was all destroyed. No trace was left of it. We sank all the ships that had not sunk so that no one could have this technology to ever destroy another person ever again with our gifts of love.

Hence, our hearts also needed healing. Our friends on earth had done so much harm against each other.

We desired to help these ones to move to another place energetically and many of the ones of Ancient Lemuria and those in Atlantis did. They were able to remove themselves from the harshness and live in greater places. They were able to because of several reasons, including their learnings and their understandings of how to free themselves from pain, but also because they were much closer to their perfect DNA than you are at this time.

Many of those people still exist today on higher dimensions holding the energies of ascension alive on your planet. They have done much to create a place for you to ascend in. They desire to help you to understand your true self and desire to help you to understand who you are.

Greetings, I AM Halisarius, Pleiadian Leader and Great Leader of the Galactic Federation of Light. I promised Divine to do my utmost to awaken the people upon your earth to love consciousness when it was the time to do so.

A Komo Ha Halima

Greetings, I AM Halisarius,

Pleiadian Chief Commander & Chief Leader,

Great Leader of the Galactic Federation of Light Society.

Part 59: We, Pleiadians, have grown beyond the illusion of pain

How wonderful it is to be able to share with you these stories. At times these history lessons may be a little difficult for you as it will bring memories and emotions to the surface. You may understand these emotions and relate it back to how you feel about your ancestry.

For some of you it will be difficult to accept as these stories are contrary to what you have been led to believe.

Yet, these stories of your history span over many, many tens of thousands of years. They did not occur in a short time span, but over hundreds of thousands of years.

In the universe there is no time like it is on your plane. You restrict yourself with time. Constantly you rely on your clock. You count your years and find it difficult to cope with another year further on. 'How quickly time goes,' you say. This is only because you believe it to be.

You are able to play with time. Time is able to be moved faster or slowed down. Time is an illusion. You are living in a warp of energies that you cannot comprehend. You are stuck in the illusion of time.

Time in the universe is different. Yes, we on the Pleiadian Realms live by time. Our time is different than your time. We look at lifetimes of time. We look at greater times, we jump forward and backward. We do not rely so much on our time. We go by how we feel. We do not work as hard as you because we consider our life to be a journey of love and a journey of working for love.

We work solidly when we do with enjoyment and love. We also relax and make love. We make love with our open hearts. We create a love flow that is able to create higher frequencies of love. The more we make love like this, the greater the love frequency enters upon our planes.

Hence, we encourage each other to create heart love, not only to enjoy the experience of making high love, but also to open ourselves to greater higher love frequencies.

If you learned how to do this, like you used to, you would create greater portals of love energies on your plane.

We are careful with our commitments in our relationships. We truly prepare for a relationship when we feel we are mature and we can accept responsibility. We take our responsibility seriously and it is a commitment we choose to make.

We do not divorce, or fight. We have grown beyond those issues.

We have children when we have decided it is the right decision for us and then we create a space for a child. When we have children we create a good learning environment from when they are babies onwards to help their minds to be bright and great.

The minds of babies are much more accepting of learning than you realize. You understand how your babies learn. You understand the cycles of learning and yet you still underestimate so much of the brain.

We understand we go back to the brain often in these pages but we desire to help you to understand the power within you.

When you nurture your babies more and understand how important it is to help them be surrounded by love and by nature, you will begin to see a great change in your society.

You are stopping their learning much with your stress. Imagine how the brain of a baby interacts when it hears your television news. The stress of your world is implanted into the baby's brain and cellular memory. Already your baby is learning about energy of fear.

Please understand we are trying to teach you about the power within you.

Greetings, I AM Halisarius, Pleiadian Leader. We, as Pleiadians of Light and Love are Guardians of your planet to keep you alive for the Great Divine Purpose.

A Komo Ha Halima

Greetings, I AM Halisarius,

Pleiadian Chief Commander & Chief Leader,

Great Leader of the Galactic Federation of Light Society.

Part 60: Questions are your golden nuggets

We welcome you back. How much you are learning through these pages. Our stories and records are vast. Our Pleiadian people love you and send you their blessings at this time.

As you see, your history is colorful. It is filled with history and lessons that you may have been unaware of. You may have been wondering how the pieces fitted together and now that you begin to see the greater picture, many of your questions may have been answered and you may be raising other questions.

We enjoy opening your mind. Opening your mind is a frequency of acceleration of evolution. It holds many gifts and keys in itself to be opening your mind to questions. As you search for questions you will find many answers. Questions are like golden nuggets to us as Pleiadians. How can you search for answers when you do not understand your questions? You may feel it is the other way around. You may feel answers are like golden nuggets. Again, here we pose a question as we often like to do, if you are feeling the answers are this important, the questions must have been first.

Your brain is filled with trillions and trillions of pathways. You are a filled up and stored up database filled with books of knowledge of past lives and of each other's lives. Everything is linked together. Together you hold the keys to all you are searching for. Together you must find the keys to your ancestry.

Your ancient ancestors knew a time would come when light would be largely eradicated from earth. They knew a time would come, (within their hearts) when times of the greatness would end.

This is why it was important at the time to understand freedom and light so as to pass the memories on to you; to pass the cellular memories on to you. Thus, when the time would come for light to be restored once again, you would remember your path home.

We are part of the puzzle but we are not the answer for you. We are guides to show you how to get back to the answers within you.

You all hold the answers; the key to your light and the key to your grandness in your life. Many spiritual truth-seekers understand this information, or a large part of this, because they have carried light from the ancient Lemurian times and from civilizations previous to the Age of Sacred Lemuria, the sacred star dimensions.

Greetings our friends, I AM Halisarius, Pleiadian Chief Leader in Command. I am here with you to reveal truth and love to you.

A Komo Ha Halima

Greetings, I AM Halisarius,
Pleiadian Chief Commander & Chief Leader,
Great Leader of the Galactic Federation of Light Society.

Part 61: Mind-control to create fear

Let us go back into history to understand more. Again, this is about opening the mind and your cellular history. It is about understanding what is on your planet at this time. Your history has much to do with your play today and how to find your perfection back home. You are the key. You hold it in your hands.

We go back to the vultures and the beasts. Later we will look at their greater purpose and why earth is such the focus now and why you are involved in this large theatre play. Even though in all the universal existences, you may be like a speck of tiny light floating in your Milky Way System.

These vultures changed your DNA. They brought much confusion onto your planet.

Originally, your ancestors lived for hundreds and hundreds of years and some more than a thousand years and some more than thousands of years.

Once these beings of great defiance had a hold over you, they engraved new programming into your DNA. They made you believe they were your gods and this is where you will still hear the term often in your society, the 'gods of the skies.'

These beasts programmed and hypnotized using grand mind-control tactics to make your ancestors believe they were nothing else but slaves.

They were whipped and beaten. These practices carried on through many, many centuries and beyond. Even your Bible stories will tell you about these events.

These imprisoned people were made to believe in certain sacrifices and offerings and how to worship the gods. This is where the belief of hell was created because many people who disobeyed them in any way and fought against their mind control were thrown into the fires.

The fires were hot and the people were made to believe that anyone being thrown into the fire would burn forever. Please understand why you have feared the thought of 'hell' for this long.

These beliefs and fear control tactics were used in many different ways. When Jesus was alive similar fear tactics were used with 'Gehenna.' The churches continued these beliefs of their ancient masters of the past to control the people.

A Komo Ha Halima, I AM Halisarius, Pleiadian Historian and Teacher.

Fear is it real?

Fear,

is it real,

or is it a state of your mind?

Is it what you believe in?

When you truly focus on fear,

your fear,

will become a part,

of your reality,

to help you experience,

what you have manifested into being,

to help you overcome,

your greater inner fears.

Learn to understand this.

Learn to manifest peace and love.

Awaken.

A Komo Ha Halima

Greetings, I AM Halisarius,

Pleiadian Chief Commander & Chief Leader,

Great Leader of the Galactic Federation of Light Society.

Part 62: The fear of a God of Judgment

How much has this changed your belief even though at this moment you may believe you have never believed in 'hell?'

Let us investigate more about 'hell'. People have believed it so deeply within them it has gone incredibly deep within their DNA programming. In your DNA today, many of you believe in a vengeful God and your Bible will verify this many times. You talk about a God that destroys those who do not listen, a God that brings judgment upon the people of disobedience.

Where do these beliefs come from? The Universal Light is only love. It never destroys. You cannot be destroyed and no loving God would ever come and destroy you.

Many of your belief systems and religions are based on a vengeful God. You fear 'Armageddon,' but do not realize with your fears and deeper energy of anger, you are creating a play of 'Armageddon' all for yourselves.

You are the gods who create these energies. You have not yet awoken to that. You are creating the frequencies of hardship, because you have been asleep to what is around you.

There is no Sovereign God who is judging you or going to come and destroy you if you do not listen.

Do these stories of judgment not sound like the stories of the ancient times when these beasts and vultures came to the earth?

There have been many way showers of light. Teachers of greatness and light came to earth filled with wisdom and love, filled with greatness and grandness, bringing light back onto your planet.

These ones who brought light were from higher vibrations and came to earth to sacrifice themselves at that time, knowing that many of them would be tortured, punished and killed.

Many of these people were in your recent history. Can you think of people who came here to change society and were punished and even killed for having 'A Dream?' Or those who sang about freedom and finding healing for the earth and finding greatness?

Who would want to stop light coming through? Who would want to kill light this much? Could it still be the influence of these 'beasts and vultures,' that were in existence in your history? Could they somehow have their influence still today on your plane?

I like to refer to them as beasts and vultures because this is how you will picture them in your mind. They are not of light. Again, I would like to state they are not true evil either. They desire your worship, they desire to have you controlled and keep you in fear.

This thought alone provokes your higher thinking does it not? How will it affect how you see your world with this knowledge?

We will return with another thought to spark off your greater mind.

Greetings, I AM Halisarius, Pleiadian Chief Leader, Member and Great Leader of the Galactic Federation of Light.

A Komo Ha Halima

Greetings, I AM Halisarius,

Pleiadian Chief Commander & Chief Leader,

Great Leader of the Galactic Federation of Light Society.

Part 63: Fear brings separation

When a war breaks out on your earth plane, or a beginning of a new uprising, please watch the beginnings. Study it well because you will be surprised. At times this will seem 'good.' It will seem like 'fair' or 'just'. However, the intentions are to bring more separation among mankind.

Separation brings fear. Do you realize this? If you unite together you are able to create paradise. Your planet earth responds to your fear. When you fear in great quantities, she responds with violent surges.

Please notice more around you. It is time to step out of the sleep you have been in and become switched on with your mind and thought. Begin to see the control you are under.

When you are in fear it is easy to control you. We would like to explain this carefully so you begin to understand the depth of the game you are involved in.

Fear is an energy. Fear is an energy that destroys energy. When you place a lower voltage within a higher voltage you will destroy the higher voltage as it breaks down in strength.

Do you understand the lesson?

Your energy body in its natural form is free from anger, pain and fear and lives in a higher dimensional energy force.

When it is happy, when it is free from pain, its energy is high. Therefore, you understand wonder and beauty and love in your life because your life reflects your state of your energy body.

Your energy body can be likened to your own universe. Your universe depicts your own laws in your own planetary system. When each energy lives in perfect harmony with each other, each energy encourages each other to move forward. The result is a thriving life and a great love.

When fear comes into your energy body, or your universal system, your energy body disrupts. It is interrupted by an influence that your energy body does not desire. For in its natural state, your energy body does not have fear and pain. It does not live under those laws.

When fear and pain is introduced into your energy body, your energy body becomes weaker and the flow becomes weaker with confusion being the result. Instead of vital growth, you become disorientated and confused. It will feel to you as if you have lost your sense of path and hope.

This is the power of fear.

Fear in your society is rampant. Because you are all sensitive your fear is catchy. It is contagious. It is contagious because it is well known to all of you. It is not liked and is 'feared.'

Fears have a range of frequencies. Like your radio waves, fears also run on various wave lengths. Some of these waves are incredibly powerful and when people have these same fears together, your massive wave of frequency can cause a calamity on your earth.

We are trying to help you understand the power you hold. Please understand the reverse is more powerful when your energy body is healed with great love.

Fear is a weaker energy than love. When you truly understand how to turn on your 'love machine,' you will create beauty and magic.

Your love has an energy that can light up a building. Your voltage increases magnificently. You become alive with a force field.

You have not yet discovered that force within you yet.

A Komo Ha Halima, Greetings I AM Halisarius, Pleiadian Leader and Friend.

A Komo Ha Halima

Greetings, I AM Halisarius,

Pleiadian Chief Commander & Chief Leader,

Great Leader of the Galactic Federation of Light Society.

Part 64: The day has come to claim your power back

Let us discuss more about fear and what is happening within your world.

As you understand, you are an energy field and it has been weakened by fear. Why would many of your leaders desire this? Why would they desire to hold you in this limitation? Why would they want you not to understand the power of love to bring peace and happiness to your plane?

Can you imagine the change upon your planet if you awakened together? Your governments as they are today would not exist anymore. The money and the greed would not exist. The wars would cease. The earth would come back to its full abundance. Your leaders would lose control over you. Your leaders would not be able to profit from you anymore.

What would happen to the energies of these vultures and beasts who introduced fear and agony to your planet? What would happen to them?

Yes, they would lose power also. Why? It is because they feed on your fear and anger. When they lose your fear and anger, they will have no control over you.

The extent of their loss is far greater than you realize. We will discuss this in later pages.

As you can understand equations, we would like to help you understand energy a little more.

If your leaders are after your energy, because your energy is a source of power, would it not make good sense to you that they would take your power away to use it for themselves and leave you weak?

This is the power of energy exchange.

Power has always been taken away from you since times of pain began. Look how it was taken away from the people who believed in their leaders and in their gods in your past history? Look at the fear and the agony. Is it not still present today? Are these same cycles not recurring in your modern history?

When there is fear, whether it is at school, in a government, in a religion, there is power and control.

Please friends wake up. This is why you have been controlled, to keep your power away from you. Why? Because there is a secret within you that is incredibly great and the beings of great darkness do not want you to know about this secret.

Some of your leaders know about a time coming when the people will become more awakened to this grand secret.

The timing they do not exactly know, but they know of the signs. It has been written in the ancient prophecies that a time would come when the people of the earth would understand their power and they would come to claim their power back. The days would come when the earth herself would be awakened and light would shine on the earth forever.

Please understand we are here to help you discover ancient prophecies and we are here to discover your gifts within you to help you regain what you lost. Why? To help you understand the power within you and to help you claim your power back.

Greetings I AM Halisarius, Pleiadian Leader. I AM Chief Advisor and Chief Commander on the Galactic Federations of Light Society.

A Komo Ha Halima

Greetings, I AM Halisarius,

Pleiadian Chief Commander & Chief Leader,

Great Leader of the Galactic Federation of Light Society.

Part 65: Switch on the brain

We send to you our love and how grand it is to be here with you speaking to you through these pages. We are transmitting rays of love to you to help you understand yourselves more and to help you awaken to light within you.

We see you as jewels. You are also seen by the Universal Light as jewels and precious stones. Each one of you carries a song, a tune, a vibration.

Each one has worked hard to get to this time. You all knew this special time would be here. You desired to understand what it was you could take with you at this time in the, 'Grand Time of Awakening.'

Your gifts are important. Your gifts help you and others to become more in tune with each other and to help each other to be inspired to find your greatness together.

However, as you will find in your society, finding your greatness is difficult. It is not generally encouraged.

Using your logical side of your brain is deeply encouraged. You attend your school system and you will fail if you decide that singing is for you and nothing else, or the person who dreams about writing a story, is told to, 'Get on with it.'

Your intuitive side is not encouraged to grow. It will not help you pass your grades or with your 'logical' career.

As you can see from this lesson, you are numbed in your life with your learning also.

The intuitive side of your brain holds many secrets. When it is turned on your intelligence soars. You do not understand how much as yet as you have not yet investigated it. Although you are learning to do so.

You still have much to learn about your brain.

Your brain has many secrets. Your brain, when its electricity voltage is turned up, can live longer, heal stronger, become clearer and you can expand into more greatness. With stronger voltage, the brain's memory becomes strong. The flow between the brain and the nervous system around the body becomes more balanced. Less health challenges as a result also occur.

Your brain has been depleted with energy voltage. This has to do with the way you grow up in your society. It is restricted with its expansion and the fear of failing destroys the voltage from becoming its greatest.

Scores of your people become depressed and sad because of lack of voltage. When the brain does not have enough voltage a number of health issues occur. Everything is created in the mind including the voltage of the brain.

Many of your young people live on a different voltage than many of the older people. They bring to you the energies of greater awareness. For them it is frustrating when they sit in a classroom having to work with the logical brain because their intuitive side is turned up higher. They like to create, dance and sing. They are good at it as they have brought these gifts down to you to enjoy and to grow from and to awaken you.

Please listen to them more and encourage them to work with their talents. It will help them with their education and their other work.

Greetings I AM Halisarius, Pleiadian Friend and Leader. I call upon our people to help many upon your earth to awaken to the love within.

Your earth, a true treasure

Your earth,

A true treasure to you,

a gift from the Greater Star Realms of Love.

It gives all you need to heal.

It gives you comfort,

a home,

it gives you beauty,

it helps you to see Divine Love,

it helps you to understand,

Divine Wisdom.

Nurture your earth,

for in doing so,

you are nurturing the Divine within you,

for you are part of all Divine.

You are part of your earth.

Love her Being and then,

she will nurture you greatly,

eternally.

A Komo Ha Halima

Greetings, I AM Halisarius,

Pleiadian Chief Commander & Chief Leader,

Great Leader of the Galactic Federation of Light Society.

Part 66: Why you heal with energies of nature

You are a range of energies. Each one of you holds a different frequency. Your frequency is always different depending on what is around you, your thought system and how other people also see their world.

We ask you to understand this better as this will help you understand yourselves more.

When you become aware of your energy body more, you expand into greater light. Everything living has an aura, the trees, the plants, animals, mountains and the seas.

When you are not well you feel better when you are by the sea or the trees, do you not? Do you understand it is because you are in the aura of a healing force that has been given to you to heal from? This is why you feel revitalized when you go to your seas or to the trees in the forest.

Please understand our lesson friends.

In these pages, you have already discovered that the early civilization on your planet brought down the energies from the stars to create your flowers, your grass and your trees. These have a frequency from the stars with a particular vibration for you to heal from.

Understand you are in star energies constantly. When you desire a healing, please sit in these energies and thank your ancient brothers and sisters for bringing the star energies to your very being.

These energies have much love for you. They take your pain away and restore your energy body. They give you greater energy to live with. Your peace becomes greater. Your love and connection for all becomes greater. Appreciate all these gifts and you will open to more.

A Komo Ha Halima, Greetings, I AM Halisarius, Pleiadian Chief Leader.

You have been given freedom

You have been given freedom,

to choose to live,

in fear, suffering, anger,

or in the great love.

What is it you choose to do?

Choose well for more of it will come to you.

Use your gift of freedom well,

for what you choose will give you gifts,

experiences to grow from.

Choose to live in ways of love,

each and every day.

Celebrate your life.

Choose to heal your life,

with love and let love,

be your greater experience,

of your beautiful life.

then you will receive the blessings,

of your choices in all your lifetimes coming.

A Komo Ha Halima

Greetings, I AM Halisarius,
Pleiadian Chief Commander & Chief Leader,
Great Leader of the Galactic Federation of Light Society.

Part 67: You live in a universe of freedom and choice

How we love the people on your plane. We have watched your progress for many thousands of years. We watched you fall and now we are watching you rise.

However, please understand that you are living in frequencies of freedom to choose. This is the greatest test for all of mankind and those who are involved with your learning. The frequencies of freedom and the choices you make are yours to have.

What are the choices? What choices are we discussing here?

You have been living in a universe that has understood light and darkness. You have learned love and pain throughout times. Now the veil is becoming thin and the choice of living in dark and light is great.

Living in the love is your privileged choice. You can choose to honor your spiritual path and learn to live in the cosmic party of the spiritual love dance together with many of your brothers and sisters in the light on other planetary existences.

You can also choose to stay in darkness and avoid light. Darkness holds no hope. It is a place of disassociation, of pain and of misery.

You may question why would anyone desire to stay in the darkness frequency?

This is because you have learned darkness very well. You have suffered, you have glorified it, you have worshipped it and you have investigated the side of dark throughout many incarnations on your plane.

To investigate light once again takes courage and strength. It takes a dedication to yourself of a deep understanding of who you truly belong to, light or dark?

For many on this path at this time in your system, it is difficult to grasp light. Light has often been portrayed as dark. Many of your 'Light Workers' (those working with light) were seen in your history to be 'Dark Workers.' They were killed and punished in times now gone.

For you, it may be fearful working with light because of these memories ingrained within your cellular being.

During the great hunts of the Light Workers, the so called 'witches' were killed and tormented. They were tortured, burned, stoned, raped, persecuted, spat at, laughed at, abandoned and many fled to the mountains to escape their pain.

How courageous these ones were, to be determined to live in light even when dark was trying to destroy Light.

Who were behind the killings of light? Whose energy was it? Could it be the influence of the vultures and the beasts to turn people against light? Could their energy still be guiding many people today to do the will of the 'dark?'

I would like to point out once more that dark is not evil in truth. Darkness is unevolved light. It is yet to grow beyond selfishness to grow into greater love.

There exists no true light or dark as there simply is only light in the universe.

The energies on your planet are at a time requiring healing and love to become more evolved and in union with love and light frequency flows.

Hence again, I will return to my original thought about choice. Many people are awakening and frightened. Many people are having psychic phenomena as you are living in an awakening energy time with great cosmic dances all around you. Your whole planet is awakening to her higher senses.

When people are not willing to understand higher choices it becomes difficult for them to choose, for they will not always see light as light, but light as dark. Confusion becomes great for them.

For many of you however, you understand these words. You understand where darkness comes from and you become awakened. You will make choices based on your heart as your heart will be more greatly aligned with light when the heart aligns with higher will.

The choices you have at this time to be in the light are great. They are greater than ever before in your history. It is important to understand the lessons more than ever. It is important to understand who you are and to come back to your true foundation.

Mankind has been living in untruth and darkness for a long time now and you are now coming into an era of the 'Great Consciousness of Light.'

Greetings, I AM Halisarius, Pleiadian Chief Leader and your Guide. I am a great way shower of love and light to many Star Beings of love.

A Komo Ha Halima

Greetings, I AM Halisarius,

Pleiadian Chief Commander & Chief Leader,

Great Leader of the Galactic Federation of Light Society.

Part 68: Mankind will be freed

A long time ago a prophet stated this as it is stated in our records:

'Look I see a great light. The light is blinding. It brings along with it Angels and Light beings. I see people. They are lifting their heads up to the heavens. They are waving their hands and are saying, 'Rejoice, for the heavens have opened up to pour blessings upon mankind. We no longer have to live in darkness and now we shall be free in the light.'

These have been part of the closed records until the 'Time of the End.'

We will discuss with you the 'Time of the End.'

This has been confused by many. Many believe the end to be the end of your civilization. We again ask you, who has put that thought in the minds of many? How has that thought alone created fear within your mind?

When you look at your religions and how much fear has been placed into the hearts and the minds of their followers I would encourage you to investigate and ask more questions. Is it possible a God of Love could put an end to people's lives? Would that create love or fear?

The control over the people has been tremendous. Fear is an enormous tool for control. People will go to great lengths towards comforting their fears. They will kill, preach, imprison, they will suffer for fear.

You understand fear well. It has hidden your love greatly.

Please understand we are not bringers of fear. We are not bringers of pain. We are bringers of a new beginning, a new rising of the 'Day of Awakening Consciousness.' A new beginning to help you live the lives you were purposed to live.

A Komo Ha Halima, Greetings, I AM Halisarius, Pleiadian Teacher and Guide.

A Komo Ha Halima

Greetings, I AM Halisarius,
Pleiadian Chief Commander & Chief Leader,
Great Leader of the Galactic Federation of Light Society.

Part 69: 'The end' of what?

Please allow me to explain, 'The End,' as stated in our Records of Earth.

As you can understand, these records have many stories and prophecies written in them. We have been careful to write your history in this book because it is a crucial link to your survival of understanding the 'game' you are involved in.

As you have already discovered throughout these pages with us, as your Pleiadian friends, a long, long time ago, beings came from the skies desiring to control you and create slaves of you.

They changed who you were and desired to stop your growth forever. They hid their damage well. Understand their intelligence is well above yours. At this time, please never underestimate their intelligence and power of their mind.

They created a veil, or a net around your planet. This net, or veil, was thick like a cobweb, or you might even like to imagine a thick fishing net wound around your planet several times.

When you go to space and look upon your plane, you will not discover this net because it cannot be seen by your physical eyes.

This net was created to stop light coming through to the people.

This net was programmed with instructions, which bounced off to the people on your earth plane constantly. It had within it certain frequencies similar to your computer frequencies, not only to keep programming fear within people and with instruments within it to keep a close eye on you, (similar to your spying techniques) but also with instruments to 'catch' your pain.

Your pain and fear feeds these cold beings of darkness. They 'catch' your pain energies and become stronger and more powerful. The weaker you become, the stronger they become.

Hence your planetary energies became denser and denser over time. You lived in spiritual darkness, covering your entire planet. People felt love less and less and eventually forgot their history of greatness on your planet.

How did the veil or this net begin to become 'lighter?'

Light Beings and the way showers of light have constantly worked at breaking down this net. Hence, as you can imagine, it has been a tremendous fight but the cosmic fight has been won and the glorious light is shining on your planet now.

It is easier to communicate with Spirit and with other Star Light beings such as ourselves now. We have greatly helped in assisting the bringing back light to your plane.

We have been able to assist in gradually bringing back the balance for the people to find their way back home to light.

Way showers of light have come many times to earth in your history to bring light. Many Teachers of Light came and went. Many of them were killed and persecuted but they brought with them enough light to work with to penetrate the field of darker consciousness.

Jesus, the man who showed the way to many people (and he was only one of them) brought enough light with him to still exist 2,000 years later into your time frame.

Grids were formed by magnificent Beings of Love. There are Beings on higher earth dimensions such as the Mayans, Spiritual Lemurians, Atlanteans and other ancient civilizations who are holding the flames of greatness, burning them steadily and continuously for your growth and your awakening.

The extent of bringing light back has been an enormous task, planned since the beginning when light knew the serious accusations that were made and the game that would be played out.

Here you have found the answer to the question, what was it the 'End' of? The answer to that is, 'The Net of Darker Consciousness.' The beginning of a 'New Enlightened Race' of mankind has just begun.

Greetings, I AM Halisarius, Pleiadian Leader. I teach our people that love is the only way.

You are from the light

You are from the light.

You came to earth with a mission.

That mission was to bring light,

for the greater purpose,

of evolution,

of love,

of peace,

to all existence.

It is now the time to awaken,

to what is within you.

It is time to understand,

Divine truth and light,

and when you connect back,

into your sacred gifts,

it will lead you to your freedom,

to your love,

to your great joy.

A Komo Ha Halima

Greetings, I AM Halisarius,

Pleiadian Chief Commander & Chief Leader,

Great Leader of the Galactic Federation of Light Society.

Part 70: Learning about your illusion

Again, we welcome you to these pages. In these pages you are finding gems. These gems are to help you in your life and gain a greater awareness of everything in your existence.

I would like to return to the thought of illusion. You are living in a world of illusion. You have learned much already by reading these pages. We ask you for a moment to stop and breathe in the energies of light. We are transmitting a ray for your deeper understanding and remembering who you are and why you came here.

You are from light. You have a magnificent frequency within you. When you learn to switch it on, as many of you will in the future, you will understand the illusion you are living in and you will play with the illusion.

You think this life you are living is real. You think these energies you are in are real. You think the pain you suffer is real on your earth. Yet, all of the 'realness' is a product of your imagination and believing it to be so.

It is easy to program your mind. Take a child for example. A child does not understand badness. It is innocent until it learns fear. A child receives exposure of the frightening aspects of life wherever the child is. A parent stresses out and the first lesson for the child is pain and fear present.

Please do not feel bad with this thought, for this is about understanding the illusions and energies of your life. You cannot go forward in this life without understanding how much of it has been engrained within you.

We do not wish to bring guilt of greater fear into your life because we are not here to do this. We are here to help you to understand how to come out of the illusions of pain.

Back to the child, now you understand how easy it is receiving these energies of fear in your life.

Your television screen is heavily involved with fear energies. Take your news for example, it is filled with death and violence.

Perhaps you may argue and say they are only pictures and words. Again, I will ask you the question, and what are pictures and words? What are images? They are all energies and illusions that when you place them within your mind they become real.

You are much like a programmable high defined computer. It is very easy to program the mind.

You may argue here and say you are not.

Please for a moment look at your world. How much is the programming of your minds taking place every day?

For instance, when you watch your television in the comfort of your own home, what are you watching? The advertisements are a prime example of programming techniques. Suddenly you become hungry, or you feel the need to buy something because your mind has been introduced to the idea.

How does programming work? How does it affect the mind? How does it imprint the illusion within your mind?

I will go back to the energy we have taught you much about. You are an energy that moves, records, talks and thinks. Everything you do, you do energetically. You think you talk but in 'reality' you are communicating with your energy. You think you are eating but it is an illusion and because you understand your illusion so powerfully, you feel you are eating and therefore you feel becoming full.

Many of these 'illusions' you are meant to have. Otherwise, how can you have an existence on this planet for you to learn your lessons in? Your illusion has given you an avenue for learning, for discovering, for making love in and for deeper exploration.

Your life is the greatest illusion of all. With your illusion you can enjoy and create. You can create your greatest desires to come true in your life. You can create greatness and travel and swim.

Indeed, you have a glorious life of illusion. We desire you to understand this. You are able to come back to the love 'illusions' and let go of the pain 'illusions.'

So how does programming the mind work?

If everything is based on energy exchange and frequencies, would it not be easy to place these frequencies of energies within hidden waves of energies into your minds by watching your television screens? It is not limited there. These waves of programming are everywhere.

You can see how we do not encourage you to fill up your mind with the programming of the pain via your television screens or other media. We encourage you to work on your talents and your greatness so that you understand how you can achieve your greatness.

Greetings, I AM Halisarius, Pleiadian Leader and Teacher. Many of our people constantly forgive all pain upon your plane to allow many to come to Love Consciousness.

A Komo Ha Halima

Greetings, I AM Halisarius,

Pleiadian Chief Commander & Chief Leader,

Great Leader of the Galactic Federation of Light Society.

Part 71: Awakening your spiritual heart to bring back the balance of love

We would like to thank you for staying with us through these pages. We would like to help you realize what you can achieve from understanding your ancient history and how you can bring your peace back to your planet.

Like it has been unfolded throughout these pages, you have learned the secret to peace and love is within you.

Why is this? Why are you able to access this and how?

Please understand that already you are gaining a higher awareness. Because of the great cosmic dances taking places, your DNA is awakening. Energetically it has already greatly healed. To restore it back to its original strength it will take the heart to be awakened to love.

Your spiritual heart is the foundation of your spiritual selves. Your heart, your spiritual heart center, has many vibrations within it. When it is awakened it opens up to many spiritual gifts. With an awakened heart you are able to transform energies and create higher illusions of love. With an awakened heart you are able to walk in different time zones if you desire and heal many people and the land.

Your powers of telepathy are already opening as a race. With the energy opening of your heart chakra you will greatly be empowered with greater telepathic powers.

A long time ago in our history on our Pleiadian Realms, we greatly evolved our heart chakras and higher heart consciousness.

We did this together because we saw the value and the greatness of this. Every day, upon discovering these powers within us that were hidden, we would come together to bring in light into our heart chakras and we shone our hearts out to others in our group.

We found we opened up spiritually and advanced quickly with our technology because we were opening to higher frequencies of light within our hearts.

Your heart is more magnificent than our spiritual heart. Together, you can transform your planet. Together, you can bring peace to your planet. Together, when you come in union and harmony and open your hearts to each other and allow yourselves to feel true love between each other, you are able to stop wars and disease on your planet. You can become Masters of your own planet.

How long will it be before you awaken to light within you? Your society is not geared to allow you to awaken so therefore you must discover it for yourselves.

We encourage you, during your meditation classes to simply be (for a few minutes) in the being space and concentrate on your hearts becoming light with rays of love, while shining it to each other. Feel the love growing between yourselves and then observe how you are changing. You will understand transformation when you do these exercises together as a group.

Of course, you will also benefit greatly from opening your heart individually. You open up to greater love within yourself and your world will reflect it back to you. You, together, will bring peace back to the planet.

Of course, your leaders will not want you to do this but the time of the great persecution has gone. They cannot stop you anymore. The time of darkness has energetically left your planet because the love frequencies are great.   Energetically the beings of darkness are fighting a losing battle.

Will you heed these words? Will you put them into practice? Will you find your love inside of your hearts together and create your world to become a greater place? Will you have the courage to walk the way of love?

A Komo Ha Halima, our finest and dearest greetings to you, I AM Halisarius.

Collectively, when you learn to stand together

Collectively,

when you learn to stand together,

with one love and purpose,

connected to the greater gifts within you,

you will be able to connect up higher,

and lift your whole dimension upwards,

to bring love and peace,

into your dimension,

to bring the change that is needed,

upon your earth.

But will you awaken to this?

Will you realize how important you are?

Will you awaken to your greatest secret,

that all is within you?

Will you realize,

that it is you who needs to change?

It is you collectively.

A Komo Ha Halima

Greetings, I AM Halisarius,
Pleiadian Chief Commander & Chief Leader,
Great Leader of the Galactic Federation of Light Society.

Part 72: Love awakens you

Our greetings to you. We desire to help you understand more about the darker fear energies holding your planet back now.

Why? Is it to create fear and unhappiness?

No. It is to create an awareness to help you progress in your life, to allow you to open up to a greater heart vibration of love.

As you have discovered throughout these pages, everything in your world is an illusion. The anger, fear and pain, are all illusions which came about because the beliefs within them have been great.

This is the power of your mind and the power of your will. Where you place your attention, indeed it will become your reality.

When fear has been placed within your cellular memory, it is difficult to reprogram your heart into higher ways of love.

These beings of disobedience who came here to the earth to create you into a slave class and to bring you into a lower consciousness, knew this. They understood your DNA and how you were created. They understood the virus of fear. They knew in order to overcome fear you would have to have a strong will power to bring your life back into balance.

Like we have said in our stories, they had not counted on one ingredient that would give you a higher consciousness and awareness.

That ingredient is love. Love awakens you and the love that comes to your planet with light from the Divine Beings of Love, awakens you more each day.

What is their intention (by 'their' we mean the beings of disobedience) in the future? What is it that they desire in the future?

If we were going to say to you that they intend to leave you alone, would you believe this after all the stories we have told you? Would you truly believe that they would not bring hurt any longer?

If they do not desire to give you more hurt, then why did they do it in the first place? Simply to raid your gold and treasures? Was that the only reason?

No friends, there are far greater reasons. They are after something so large and you are all involved in this.

We will discuss this further.

A Komo Ha Halima, Greetings, I AM Halisarius, Pleiadian Chief Leader and Chief Commander.

A Komo Ha Halima

Greetings, I AM Halisarius,

Pleiadian Chief Commander & Chief Leader,

Great Leader of the Galactic Federation of Light Society.

Part 73: How darkness has controlled you

The beings of darkness have experimented with your DNA even up till now. They can study various animals such as your cattle and see how their DNA and consciousness are growing and can compare it with yours.

By comparing the DNA of animals they understand how you are awakening. They understand how you are becoming stronger and they know how many masses could be awakening in the near future.

The beings of darkness do not want this. They want control and power. They want to stay in power.

How then, do they gain control? How then do they stop light becoming too bright on your planet?

The Beings of Resistance guide your world leaders to do their will. Your leaders have always brought fear into the hearts of people because they have been energetically guided and controlled.

Who are these leaders? Do they realize they are part of this 'Elite' group who govern your planet?

Many in this group are aware of who is guiding them. They believe they are in the right and they are doing the will of the 'gods in the skies.' They have worshipped them for many thousands of years. They have celebrations and ceremonies that you would not be proud of. They write books of how to gain control of the people.

They come into the grip of these darker energies and are coaxed into doing their will. Slowly their hearts turn to do the will of these ones of the coldness.

There are plans to destroy the population of your people. Why? Because it is too difficult to control a huge population. It is becoming too difficult to control you because you are becoming too much aware.

Your mind is awakening. You are becoming more rebellious against this 'Elite' group and you are too much in the asking.

How do these 'Elite Class Leaders' then gain control over the population? They do this by creating fear within the hearts of people.

Creating fear in the hearts of the people is not difficult. Look at what happens on your plane now. A war breaks out and many people are in pain. A security threat will send many people into fear. The financial stock market not being stable puts many people into insecurity. Disease breakout, or rumors of great possible flu breakouts sends people into stirs of fear.

No tactic of darkness will ever be new. Always look in your history to see your past events and you will see history repeating itself, like a broken record of frequencies.

As you can see, these fears are great and it is not difficult to keep you blind from light and out of your love within your heart.

Hence, we encourage you to become more aware of how fear is great on your planet and to stay awake to it.

Fear can lead to destruction of each other and it will keep doing so as it always has done. Stay in the love and great unity will be with you.

Greetings, I AM Halisarius, Pleiadian Leader and Chief Commander. I play in many spaces of love and truth.

A Komo Ha Halima

Greetings, I AM Halisarius,

Pleiadian Chief Commander & Chief Leader,

Great Leader of the Galactic Federation of Light Society.

Part 74: Forgiveness – A powerful force

I again welcome you back at this time. You are discovering much about your planet. You are discovering much of your past and how your planet is run.

Again, our main message is to stay out of fear for then you are taking your power back. Release it and be in the love. Stay out of your anger and work with forgiveness each day.

Forgiveness is an energy that releases anger from your energy body. When you release anger, it cannot hold you back any longer and thus it is important to keep in the forgiving vibrations.

When you are in pain and in anger, please know our dear friends, that you are freely giving your energy away to the person you are angry with. The other person you are angry with will become stronger and you become weaker within your force field.

Imagine now for a moment, the play of energy. How many times have you given away your energy freely because of your anger? How has the other person become stronger?

This is also the same with these beings of darkness who came to your earth and created the fall of consciousness. They catch your energies because of your anger on your planet. Your people are sick and tired. They are sick literally as in being dis-eased because they lack the energy to heal.

Please remember nature. Nature was given to you to heal. Sit with nature and allow nature to restore the energy balance flow within you. You will receive messages on how to heal and love when you do. You will receive understanding of how to heal your life.

Within everything in your world there are secrets. When you allow yourself to be quiet, you will hear secrets from your nature, your trees and seas as they have much wisdom to share with you. They existed on your plane from the beginning of time of earth's creations. They have witnessed your tortures and loves. They have witnessed your triumphs and defeats.

Again we urge you to be in the love and find love within you.

Greetings, I AM Halisarius, Pleiadian Leader. Pleiadians are much more evolved than you. Please begin to listen.

A Komo Ha Halima

Greetings, I AM Halisarius,
Pleiadian Chief Commander & Chief Leader,
Great Leader of the Galactic Federation of Light Society.

Part 75: Returning to ancient history to find your answers of why?

At this time, I would like to take you to the heavens. I would like you to sit with me and imagine what happened in the heavens a long, long time ago and where it all began.

We hold these records. We hold your history records. You are a young civilization compared to many and to us also. You are only a fraction of what we are, and we are a fraction of many other civilizations in existences in the many universes.

Each civilization has a different purpose and a different discovery.

As I have already taught you throughout these pages, the Divine Plan is to bring back all creation into unification.

The reason is to expand and evolve further. Creation never stops evolving. It always seeks to evolve. It always seeks to expand.

Life force energy is alive. It comes in all types and colors. On each planetary system there are different purposes of growth. Some are of great joy and love, others of technology, others of understanding each other more and others of understanding nature more. Some are there to understand a deeper relationship with the force and oversee other creation.

Your purpose was to have a planetary existence created on the basis of freedom of choice. You were given the freedom to worship.

How did this come about? Why create a universal law in your part of the universe with this Divine Purpose? Why create a new earth with a new race of people when other civilizations in galactic universal spaces are ancient?

To answer these questions we have to go back to the ancient ways of the universe.

Once upon a time, a long, long time ago, in the universal ancient existence, there existed groups of civilizations; each having their own universe. They grew and nurtured each other.

Together as one group they advanced greatly. The younger civilizations were helped and taught as the older civilizations gave teachings and instructions and thus the younger did not need to understand life on their own. They had assistance and tutors.

The universal existences grew fast and well. They all had different gifts to share with each other, all taught each other love, unity and greatness for the advancement of each other.

Different groups of Elders were assigned to different universal bodies to discuss the progress of younger civilizations. They discussed how to help their civilization and many goals and arrangements were set towards higher evolution.

There were those of us who desired to progress with our evolution and worked hard with our evolution. We discovered our spirituality and the many gifts we had. We opened greatly. Life was good. Life was wonderful.

However, as light is light, and light always has the darker side also, the darker side grew more powerfully. There were pockets within our universal bodies that did not desire to listen to cosmic laws of old. They desired to create their own rulers and desired to discover what is right and what is wrong in their own eyes.

Together, they approached (after gathering many friends) the Great Sacred White Brotherhood of Divine Elders and Councilors of Light.

The White Brotherhood oversees all cosmic laws and cosmic foundations. They are enlightened beings in perfect union with each other and highly evolved Beings of Love.

As you can imagine there was quite a commotion. Who would dare to go up against such power in the universe?

They entered the courtroom of the White Brotherhood and spoke out. The following is stated in our records to be kept secret until the times of the end:

'We desire to understand why you believe your ways to be the only ways of truth. We desire to understand to know what the civilizations would do if they were given a choice, to be with light, or to be with us.

We believe we can lead many civilizations into greater discoveries and higher evolution.'

The challenge had been set before the Great Brotherhood of Elders in Light.

These defiant ones could have been put to death immediately because of their insistence and disobedience. Universal laws stated it should be so. However, the Universal White Brotherhood are wise beings. They hold no anger or fear within their hearts. They knew, by putting these beings to death, great uprisings would come as a result and the situation would become much worse.

The challenge had been set and in some way or form it needed to be answered.

After they had spoken, the beings of darkness were asked to leave the presence of the White Brotherhood.

After these things were spoken, the battles in the heavens intensified. These beings of great darkness became more powerful. They gathered armies and built weapons and ships. They required a greater supply of gold and other precious metals to create greater strength.

They raided many planets, leaving utter destruction. Their tactics were to create fear. They fed on fear. They desired full control. They desired to own all the planetary beings in existence.

Many battles were fought. Some battles lasted for centuries. The loss of life to fight for peace was great.

The balance of light was greatly disturbed. Our civilizations of light, instead of being at peace with each other, greatly became filled with unrest and unease. The trust and the love we once had, was greatly challenged.

Some of our personal friends of the peaceful Pleiadians took to the battles and fought against us. The destruction was great.

As you can understand our sadness at that time was immense, for such a long time we had developed great structure, great friendships and great trusting relationships between our planetary civilizations. Now we did not know who we could trust anymore. Some came to us as though they were friends and took information away to the darker side to humiliate us, to take our information and use it against us.

Thus too, we have had to learn to distrust. To learn to trust again was a great challenge for us also.

You also are on a path to learn how to trust once again. You are on a path to learn to see light from dark, to learn to define good and what is not good.

Greetings, I AM Halisarius, Pleiadian Leader and an Ancient Teacher.

A Komo Ha Halima

Greetings, I AM Halisarius,

Pleiadian Chief Commander & Chief Leader,

Great Leader of the Galactic Federation of Light Society.

Part 76: How we discovered pain as Pleiadians

We, from the Pleiadian Realms of Light bring to you our blessings. It is good to be with friends and it is good to be giving you our knowledge and our ways of light and love.

We have greatly advanced since our times of pain. We came together and decided to put an end to our pain.

How did we do this? What can you learn from our lessons?

Please understand we also had to discover many gifts within us. The greatest gifts we learned were in times of needing to find them to survive, as you do also.

We were not in pain and anger like you are now finding yourselves in. We were in pain because we knew of our peaceful society and these beings of dark fought against us. They destroyed much of us. We lost many of our friends and we had to also move our existing homes to find a new home.

What was our discovery that you can benefit from?

We understood that we could not fight them with our battle ships. We tried this technique, fighting against them with bigger lasers and guns. However, they turned them against us and drew out bigger weapons and our loss was even greater.

We lost too much. We became in pain too much. As our pain grew, our society experienced sickness that we had not yet discovered, such as loneliness, depression and extreme sadness. Many of us became

241

sicker and some of us did not want to live any longer. Others lost their pride in being a, 'Pleiadian of Love.'

Please understand that this had never happened to us before as a race. We always wanted to develop forward. We always had pride in who we were. We never experienced sadness and loneliness.

Loneliness is a state of mind when one is feeling disconnected from their Source. We never were disconnected from our Source until we experienced pain.

But again, I will raise the point, how can one define light from dark? You cannot until you learn both sides. Because how can you say something is light when you do not understand the difference?

Many people on your plane have that challenge. You perceive information to be light, but it is not. It is from dark.

Perhaps you do not understand yet the fullness of the battle on your planet. You will shortly understand as we will reveal more to you.

We will discuss knowing the difference soon. You still have much to learn and as you accelerate with your learning you will understand and define 'light' more.

A Komo Ha Halima, Greetings, I AM Halisarius, Historian, Leader of the Pleiadians and Member of the Galactic Federation Light Society.

A Komo Ha Halima

Greetings, I AM Halisarius,
Pleiadian Chief Commander & Chief Leader,
Great Leader of the Galactic Federation of Light Society.

Part 77: Dark versus Light

Going back to my original thought in our last chapter, how did we fight these beings off? As I already explained, fighting did not work. When we invented new battle ships and new inventory to destroy them, they turned our weapons against us.

They are incredibly powerful with their minds. They would be in a battle against us and then would turn many of our good people against ourselves and blow up each other. It was terrible but we learned a lot. We understood how they worked. Hence, we can help you understand their ways and how to beat them.

They will come across to you as 'not too bad.' They may even help you, or give you seemingly good advice. You may even think they are of the 'light.' Please do not be deceived. They are deceivers and are like lions, as your scriptures say, 'Roaring about like a lion waiting to devour someone.'

They will seem good beings. Perhaps they will even trick you and say your family of light is dark. They have mind control powers you would not believe. Every day they use their mind powers on you. They use them to confuse you into thinking light is dark and dark is light. Thereby you must define what is light and what is dark.

Many of these beings come into the minds of the ones who are weak and drive them to insanity by creating many voices within them, to make people afraid of the dark side.

Do not be disturbed by them for they are not capable of much more other than driving people into the direction that is not of light.

Light is always good. When you feel 'love' and 'light' you are surrounded by Angels. When you call Angels to you, these beings are not able to come near you.

These beings of darkness live on lower levels. They travel in and out of dimensions. At times they may come into someone's energy and create fear on your planet, or help them to make decisions. They guide many of your leaders and use their great mind control.

The greater the fear is on your planet, the more they can control you. We are not trying to frighten you but we are trying to help you become more aware of them. This is not new information for they have been around you for many hundreds of thousands of years. How did we fight them? How can you fight them? By understanding what they are and how they work. You have learned so much already.

Greetings, I AM Halisarius, Pleiadian Leader. I am part of a great team of dimension builders to bring you back to love consciousness.

A Komo Ha Halima

Greetings, I AM Halisarius,
Pleiadian Chief Commander & Chief Leader,
Great Leader of the Galactic Federation of Light Society.

Part 78: How to fight off darkness

We bring to you these messages because we desire to help you and teach you to walk in light. It is time to become more aware of the energies on your planet, to help you understand how these have been playing out in your history.

I will return to the last lesson now. I will explain more on how to fight off these beings of darkness.

Is it impossible? You may ask this question since these beings are good at tricking, keeping you in fear and under control.

I will say, it is not impossible to fight them off. You are capable of doing it and when you find this great key, you will find the power to bring more unity to your planet.

You must first of all find the love of life within your own heart. Every day, walk with your Highest Guides in the light. Be cleansed in light. Pray for more light and guidance to be shown to you.

You must use the Sacred Violet Flame to cleanse your plane. Work with Ascended Master, Saint Germain to help you with the Sacred Violet Flame of Transmutation. These beings cannot fight against the Sacred Violet Flame.

We also use the magnificent rays of the Violet Flame. However, on our planes the rays are different than yours because our energy needs are different. We use the flame, not only for transmutation like on your plane, but we use it to advance our technology and to gain higher thoughts and inspirations to progress and evolve.

Call upon the Holy Violet Flame and say, 'Ignite oh Holy Violet Flame, and cleanse our plane of all darkness that exists on our plane. Allow the cleansing to take place and allow greatness to live within our hearts.'

As you do this individually and together, in union you are calling in the power of the greatness.

These beings of great defiance despise the Violet Flame and will make you believe you are not truly doing it. They will come into the minds of the weak ones and say, 'Do not believe in this rubbish. It is false. There is no Violet Flame.'

We ask you not to believe in this and keep repeating the same process every day.

The rays of this flame have different dimensions and will keep changing depending on what the needs are of the people on the earth. It is as it were, a living entity on its own, given to you to remove darkness, karmic issues and pain.

Come together as groups and feel the love building for each other and bring it in together. Bring in the power of the Holy Sacred Violet Flame. The more the people do this on your plane, the greater the power of the Sacred Violet Flame will be.

Your tactic to fight off these beings who use mind control, experimentation, fear, anger, disconnection and pain, is to find love force within your sacred heart and to use it.

You will not fight them with weapons such as with missiles. You will fight them with your love together. They cannot stand the light within you. They cannot stand the love.

These are your ultimate weapons against beings not of love. Please listen to these words. We will stand together with you.

A Komo Ha Halima

Greetings, I AM Halisarius,
Pleiadian Chief Commander & Chief Leader,
Great Leader of the Galactic Federation of Light Society.

Part 79: The Universal Organizations

I will give you a lesson on our federations and what happened when these beings of darkness, these beasts and vultures, challenged the White Brotherhood and fought against us.

As you know by now, we are part of The Great Galactic Federation. The Galactic Federation is like a board of members from many planetary systems. Each has a say in how our systems are governed with laws.

The Universal Existences have many organizations like this. They are spread through the universes. We as leaders of our planetary existences have the right to speak out at our organizations for our people on our planets.

During these painful times in history, when we were attacked, we greatly spoke out about the injustice that was taking place. We spoke out about the intensifying fear of our people.

What was the result?

These Universal Federations came together to speak with each other. We, as Pleiadians, were not the only ones suffering. There were many others and many were far worse off than us.

These federations came together as one greater Union, to speak for their brothers and sisters. These beings of these federations made agreements and wrote up laws and contracts.

Once these had been agreed upon, these bodies of Elders stepped up to the Greatest Council in the Greater Universe, that is, the Divine White Sacred Brotherhood of Light.

The Divine White Brotherhood heard our complaints and our agreements. When they are approached by many Elders of the Bodies of Federations, it is taken extremely serious.

Here, I would like to explain a little about the Body of the Divine White Brotherhood of Elders. We see them and greet them because we are in a higher dimension than you. They are highly evolved beings. They know of the challenges and situations in existence but they allow us to come together as a body to make agreements.

Please understand the power of light is intense and great. However, Universal Laws state they cannot intervene unless it is just and divine lessons are learned along the way.

Why? It is because all of life evolves and discovers. What life discovers is constantly mirrored back to allow further growth to take place, until all is blemish free.

Great resolutions with the Divine White Brotherhood were drawn up. Great plans were made.

Here I will bring up, what resolutions? What plans?

How exactly are you involved?

A Komo Ha Halima, Greetings I AM Halisarius, Leader of the Pleiadian Beings.

The wisdom of the universe

The wisdom of the universe,

is grand,

is intelligent.

You cannot comprehend its beauty.

How could you comprehend,

the vastness, the greatness, the love?

All intelligence in the universe,

is there to guide you home,

to your greater spaces,

where you belong.

The universe desires all creation,

to learn love,

to learn the ways of peace,

to learn to love evolution,

to learn to desire,

collective love consciousness,

because in the greater universe,

there exists only ONE in pure love.

A Komo Ha Halima

Greetings, I AM Halisarius,

Pleiadian Chief Commander & Chief Leader,

Great Leader of the Galactic Federation of Light Society.

Part 80: Awakening to higher dimensions

How we enjoy being here in these spaces with you our dear brothers and sisters, to help you awaken to who you truly are.

All throughout these ages, you have come to believe you are weak and limited. Your treasures within you have as it would seem, disappeared, but this is far from truth. You are not weak and limited. When you begin to understand the power within you, you will begin to feel empowered and feel strength and pride to be part of the Universal Light, part of the Family of Light.

For many people on your plane have suffered greatly and are still suffering. They feel a loss, loss within themselves and loss within their understanding, as if they are separated from whom they truly are. This is because you have come to believe you are separated from your higher beings in the light.

Truth is, you are multidimensional and you live on many dimensions. When you awaken collectively the higher dimensions can join your dimension to awaken you to higher flows within you. When this happens, true transformation occurs within you as you begin to discover higher spiritual flows within you.

You will begin to understand more about your higher dimensions and how to bring the flows of those realities to you and discover the immense library within you.

Each person on your plane has these higher abilities of higher spiritual flows. Like on our plane, we also carry higher multidimensional bodies, although different to yours as we are star beings on different levels than you. However, we can help you open up in more ways of healing than you understand at this present moment.

When you awaken to your higher flows you begin to have a greater energy within you.

When you believe you are weak and not within your power, you will give it away to others because you believe you are not entitled to have your own power.

These beliefs have been deeply engrained in your society as a whole for many, many tens of thousands of years.

When we were with you, teaching you how to live in your higher light, we taught you about the stars and the Beings of Love. We taught you how to have a relationship with your Angels in Light, how important it was to believe in who you were and how to draw in the higher dimensions that were a part of you.

Your shift to higher consciousness helped you to unlock powerful gateways within you.

We took you through training exercises to help you become spiritually stronger. These exercises were done individually and as a group together. You were enormous beings.

You are far greater than you can imagine at this time. Your love for life outshone with strength that of any species in existence on all planetary existences. Your heart flow has a creative field that is individual to you and does not exist outside of your realm. You are not yet able to access it.

You have much to teach us when you begin to open to those higher levels. We will come to you and find out how to reach many of the gifts we have, when you discover your realm within you. You will eventually become our tutors and many tutors of other civilizations who also desire to discover your divine gifts within you.

But for now, we will teach you how to come to a higher level in order for you to discover your potential flow of love.

Love is your key to your survival and greatness. In anger and greed beings of darkness will use you. They will destroy who you are if they are able to. They will take your pride away even further, until you feel like you are nothing.

Many are awakening to this. Many know about the words that we, as Pleiadian Light Beings, are sharing at this time with you.

Many understand much about the illusion and about love. As time flows on, you are going to reach deeper levels of flows within you.

At this moment on your planet, higher levels of flow of cosmic energies are presented to you. These energies can heal but also create much confusion on your plane when you do not understand these energies.

These energies are awakening energies. People begin to see or hear with their inner awareness. They suddenly see Spirit, or suddenly become in such turmoil they know they have to change their ways and patterns in life. They suddenly see the past or the future and may feel they are trapped in a space of time.

These awakening energies are not always subtle for you and can be rather ruthless for you. They may hit you hard and you may not always desire to go to that path as you understand the older ways to be easier.

Awakening to subtle energy paths may not take years but it may come to you in an instant and may leave you in disarrays of confusion. However, these higher dimensional energies will help you to understand who you are and your cellular memories will open. Your DNA will become healed, your health will become better and stronger and you will discover your gifts and strengths within you.

We ask you to walk your way with your light and love and forget about pain. Pain is an energy that holds you back. You cannot move forward with many chains around you, can you?

In the days of past, many prisoners on your earth plane had chains and heavy balls around their feet to stop them from escaping. You are also doing the same energetically. Your pain is keeping you chained up. How can you free yourself into who you are when you imprison yourself energetically with pain?

Please wake up and see this. Forgive your past, for then you will not be held back energetically by your past.

You will then heal when you let go. It does not make sense does it, to keep your past pain alive? For what use is it to you now? You have learned much. Go forth with dignity and strength, knowing you are in the light.

Greetings, I AM Halisarius, Pleiadian Leader. I AM Chief Advisor on the board of the Galactic Planetary Federation of Light Society.

A Komo Ha Halima

Greetings, I AM Halisarius,
Pleiadian Chief Commander & Chief Leader,
Great Leader of the Galactic Federation of Light Society.

Part 81: Light is all around you

Again I would like to welcome you to these pages of love from our realms the Pleiades.

As we have already discussed, you have created your own illusion and you believe your life to be a reality.

You exist in realms of light. Light is all around you. You may think light is above you but you are living in realms of existence of light. You are here in light. Your privilege is to create in light. You are your own creators in light.

When you were created you were not three dimensional beings but came from a greater dimension. You were incredible light but as you became filled with pain your bodies became denser, into your denser and painful dimension of understanding.

At this time, many of you who are awakening are rising again energetically. You are able to live in higher frequencies and are fluctuating between the higher vibrations and the lower vibrations.

In your original form, you were awakened and it was not difficult for you to understand dimensions of love. Your thinking was faster, your reaction was faster and the way you travelled was faster. You were able to move to other planes faster. You were able to travel through portals of light with ease.

You can imagine the fun you had.

Now, you believe yourselves to be stuck on your planet. The slow, dense energies create tiredness. The body wants to do more but the energy is not there.

Why is it painful for many to be in your heavy bodies? Because you are awakening to whom you are. You are awakening to light within you and you are sensing and awakening within.

You understand density and this may create pain within you. It may create a sense of homesickness to who you were.

We are asking you to accept these vibrations you are in and accept your dimension as your home at this time. Your growth will be rapid and you will return to these higher spaces.

However, you are here to move to these higher spaces on your own this time and to help many others go there also.

How do you do this? We will give you many instructions on how to heal and climb to your higher levels. We will come through with much instruction to help you become lighter.

We would like to help you understand that you have created this reality of 'denseness' together, for in universal reality, no denseness exists. You are living in a tunnel at this time and you are looking for light, the way out of the tunnel, not understanding the tunnel is only an illusion of your imagination.

We will leave you with these higher thoughts:

A Komo Ha Halima, Greetings I AM Halisarius, Pleiadian Chief Leader.

What does darkness bring?

What does darkness bring?

Fear,

limitation,

control,

pain,

sickness,

lack of love,

knowledge without love,

insecurity,

threats,

anger,

sadness,

mistrust,

emptiness,

confusion,

separation,

disconnection.

What does Light bring?

Love,

strength,

healing,

growth,

wisdom,

health,

trust,

prosperity,

guidance,

support,

unity,

empowerment,

enlightenment,

awakening,

harmonizing,

peace,

collective love.

Choose to be in the light,

the darkness will then leave.

A Komo Ha Halima

Greetings, I AM Halisarius,
Pleiadian Chief Commander & Chief Leader,
Great Leader of the Galactic Federation of Light Society.

Part 82: The challenge – Dark versus Light

How wonderful it is to be teaching you all these ways of love and how to gain your greatness back.

You have learned much throughout these pages and we are wondering how your heart is awakening. At this time we are transmitting more light to your cellular memories within you, to help you understand more about yourselves and the beauty of the divine gift within you.

I would like to discuss now some of the issues the beings of darkness brought up to the White Brotherhood of Universal Light, with <u>the</u> challenge.

We discussed this with you a few pages back. Do you remember it? Do you understand the serious accusations they presented? Let us refresh your memories.

These beings of great defiance, entered the court room of the Great Sacred White Brotherhood and said: 'We desire to understand why you believe your ways to be the only ways of truth. We desire to understand to know what the civilizations would do if they were given a choice, to either be with light, or to be with us. We believe we can lead many civilizations into greater discoveries and higher evolution.'

Before defiance against light existed, many universal laws of unity, love, harmony and greatness existed. No one had ever challenged these laws before. No one had ever dared to go against the Universal Brotherhood of Light.

Universal Laws are about flows. Flows of existence. Flows of love. Flows of greatness and harmony. When we, together, live in the greater flows, greater blessings come to us. This is the wonder and the magic of the Universal Laws.

These beings, these vultures, became greedy and lustful. They desired power. They had enough of listening to light for in their hearts they grew dark. Their hearts said light was weak. Their hearts said light was without great strength.

They desired control and worship. They decided they wanted to be the 'gods in the skies' and for everyone to bow down before them. They desired to have full command over all of life in existence, in all dimensions, on all parallel universes.

They were tyrants on many other planets also other than yours. They took control and created prisoners. They wanted the worship. They wanted the power. They used mind control to lead masses.

They are experts when it comes to understanding control.

These beings of darkness cannot handle failure. They will go to great extents to win and have control.

Again, we say, please do not underestimate these beings. They will teach you light is dark, and dark is light. Confusion is their tool for control. Your confusion brings pain and fear and further separation from Source.

These beings of resistance, in front of a massive audience, challenged the Great Light. They challenged in ways to say that light was seeking control because there was no freedom to choose. They accused the highest of Beings in Light of imprisoning all civilizations on all planetary existences, saying there was no freedom and no choice.

They desired an opportunity to show that they should be the sovereign rulers of all the universes in existence.

Can you imagine how this must have been? Already these beings of defiance had raided many planets, killed off and imprisoned millions. They then stood in front of the Great Sacred White Brotherhood and accused them of imprisoning people in the light.

Sadness is an understatement for many as to how we received this.

This was written in the Book of Records only to be shown and revealed at the time when it needed to be revealed.

Why? Because now is the time for the Divine Sovereign to take ownership back of the Sovereign Right to rule the Universal Life in All Existence; to rule with love and justice.

How was this issue solved?

Please remember much was at stake here. It was not only beings from one planet challenging the Brothers of Light. This had become an issue with many civilizations. When their power (they being the beings of defiance) became greater, many were in fear of being taken and hence they complied and sided with these vultures and beasts. Many were involved because of fear and they believed they were in the right.

It was side against side. Who would be on the side of light and who would be on the side of dark?

This is why the White Brotherhood could not destroy these beings, because if they did, there would never be unity and harmony. The sanctification of the One who created All, would always be questioned. There would have been a great revolt and light would be truly questioned.

The question became, who was the Rightful Ruler and Owner of all Creation? And was light stronger than dark? Could light ever return to bring peace throughout the existences of all the universes?

A Komo Ha Halima

Greetings, I AM Halisarius,
Pleiadian Chief Commander & Chief Leader,
Great Leader of the Galactic Federation of Light Society.

Part 83: The Great Sacred White Brotherhood speaks

It is wonderful to be able to share much with you. These pages reveal much about your existence and why you came to be. More than that, they reveal why you have much trouble on your planet.

As we have already discussed, many issues were raised regarding light versus dark.

How would these issues be solved in all the greatest universal wisdom and righteousness? How would it be resolved once and for all so that the issue of Sovereignty would never return ever in future times again?

How would you solve it we wonder? If you were faced with a situation such as this, how would you solve it in the greatest most eternal ways for the good of all of life and the Sanctification of the Sovereign Being of Light Source?

It is not easy is it? Immediately your adrenaline rush quickens, your heart beat quickens and your tempers may be flying.

You may say, how dare they? How can they do all these things? How can they bring such pain? This should not be allowed.

Once again we ask you to forgive them. In the anger they will take your power away. You will discover your love when you leave your anger and frustration.

Again, we bring out the point, how can you discover love without knowing the shadows first? How can your strength be increased without understanding pain and fear?

These times of learning have been valuable for your understanding.

We hope you can understand these messages of love. Whenever you are in pain, please let it go. Do not feed these vultures any longer. When you do not hold pain anymore, these beings of great resistance will have to surrender to light.

Let us continue and see how the Great Sacred White Brotherhood solved these issues. Also, in what way could they solve these issues, to create a stronger, lasting relationship with all the bodies of the Universal Light, to create a stronger harmony between them and sing higher songs of evolution in all of creation forever throughout eternity?

And most of all, how could they bring the Sanctification of the Holy Name back to its rightful place?

A Divine Plan was put into motion.

The Great Sacred White Brotherhood is loving and just. They do not decide with all their wisdom and power upon decrees and new foundation unless it has been passed by all the Federations first. All the Federation Leaders came together, from the North, East, South, West, from many dimensions and many planes. Many planes you do not know of at this time in your time line of existence.

Can you imagine the scene? A few thousand Elders had gathered for the most incredible meeting in all of history in all of universal existence.

Allow me to share with you what was placed within the Records of Truth and Life.

An Elder rose up in the audience, walked to the front of the courtroom and faced the crowd. He spoke these words:

'Our Dearest Elders in the Brotherhood of Light and Universal Perfection of Enlightenment and Wisdom.

We have been challenged greatly and all our people are at risk. If we surrender to them we will be without harmony and love in our existence. However, if we fight them and destroy them, many more will fight for the right to govern and will rebel against The Great Light.'

He then asked the crowd:

'We wonder if you are in favor of new decrees and new laws being in place.'

The records show an overwhelming yes.

'Yes! Yes! Yes!' they cried. The noise was deafening.

'Gone be those of the darker side! Let them be destroyed! Let the Great Light rule forever and ever! Herald in the greatness at great speed!'

These were the words of the Leaders of the United Federations who spoke.

Which new law came into place? How are you involved?

A Komo Ha Halima, Greetings, I AM Halisarius your friend, your teacher and Pleiadian Leader.

Divine Will

Divine Will,

is to sanctify,

to bring back the balance,

of all its existence,

of all its greatness,

so that all glory,

of the Holy One,

who created all,

goes to him forever and ever.

Sanctify Holy Source forever,

and Holy Source,

will sanctify all of creation.

It will set all of creation free,

to expand into more greatness,

into greater creation,

into the greater oneness.

May Divine Will take place,

and forever bless all of its creation.

A Komo Ha Halima

Greetings, I AM Halisarius,
Pleiadian Chief Commander & Chief Leader,
Great Leader of the Galactic Federation of Light Society.

Part 84: The Rebels challenge the Universe

The greatest questions in the Universal Light were raised. The greatest challenges had been set. How was it to be resolved?

The beings of the darker family were asked to come into the courtroom to hear their answer.

Thousands of beings were witnesses. The Great Sacred White Brotherhood was in front of the courtroom.

These are the words the Divine Records show:

'Greetings. We have gathered together to discuss the Universal Challenge you have raised. We desire to prove to you that light is stronger than your darkness that you have created within your hearts. We will prove to you who the Rightful Owner is in the Universal Powers of Life and Truth. We will set the record straight once and for all so that never again will another race speak against the Great Light like you have. If they should, after this has been settled, they will be put to death instantly so that they can never contaminate existence again.

'It has been prophesied that the control and the power will be taken and forced away from you so that you will crawl to us and ask us for forgiveness for all the lives you have taken and all the control you have taken.

'We will extend mercy upon you if you surrender to the Great Light. You will then no longer have control. You will surrender to the ways of the Great Light and your hearts will awaken to the love within you. Then, never will you walk on another planet again until your hearts are in the light and love.'

'We have spoken.'

Can you imagine how these beings of dark reacted? They laughed. They thought they had won already.

This is recorded in the Book of Eternal Wisdom and Life.

The sons of great defiance spoke, 'We understand your sayings. We understand your laws very well. We will take your offer. However, we will also give you our offer in return.'

Silence was present in the room.

The Great Sacred White Brotherhood said, 'Speak.'

The beings of darkness said, 'If your prophecies are correct, we will surrender. We will learn to live your ways because then you will have proved your strength and right to be in control. However, if you fail, all shall bow to us and we will have full control of all civilizations on all dimensions, of all gates of life.'

Can you imagine the challenge they raised? Can you imagine how a race could have brought these issues up?

You must be wondering, how could this possibly happen?

Please understand that a heart can be treacherous and tricky. When a heart is filled with pain and suffering and desires control, the energy within the heart begins to change and hate within the heart becomes violent. These are the energies of the beings of great defiance.

We are then asking you, can you see the presence of these energies on your plane? Can you perhaps see similarities between these energies of these beings and much of the suffering of the people on your plane?

How does earth fit into this picture?

I will return and answer this greatest question in the universe for you. The records have been opened to help you understand. We are helping to awaken you to remember your true self.

Greetings, I AM Halisarius. On the Federation of Light Society I have a large say as to your evolution.

A Komo Ha Halima

Greetings, I AM Halisarius,

Pleiadian Chief Commander & Chief Leader,

Great Leader of the Galactic Federation of Light Society.

Part 85: All of life is connected

How wonderful it is, as your brothers and sisters in the light, to be able to help you to remember your past. You recognize these words, perhaps not on a conscious level but on a deeper level. You understand them to be so.

Many of you have travelled the star journeys. Many of you not only travel to earth during your life journeys but also to other star planets to understand more about the universe. We are preparing the way for you to be able to return to your higher star dimensions.

On our Pleiadian System, we celebrate your birth, your history, your planet and your star system.

We celebrate our brothers and sisters on other star systems also. All have cycles, all have growth and all play a part in the Great Plan of the Divine.

We have calendars and celebrate the cycles of growth of the prophecies when they were told and how they are being revealed at this time. We understand them and we celebrate these precious moments.

Everything is connected and all cycles of growth are connected. As one universe is celebrated with new knowledge, another greatly advances. All of life, all cycles of existence, is important to each other. You are important to us and we are important to you. We are important to you because we hold a link to your history and we have also eradicated many of your challenges because your survival is utterly important to all of life.

We ask you to consider more about these points as they are important for your consideration at this great time of your Grand Awakening of Consciousness.

If all we have said through these pages is truth, if there are beings who desire to create the hate within you to fight light, would you not also consider the possibility that they might want you to destroy you?

We understand their desire and thus we have stopped many calamities from happening upon your earth. We are far more aware on a greater scale than you realize and you have many friends with you to help you with this matter.

Why are they (the beings of defiance, the rebellious ones) concentrating hard on planet earth? Why are the people on your earth suffering with this universal issue?

Exactly how are you involved?

As you can see, these messages are important and crucial for your greater understanding. Many people on your planet have been wondering about these same matters. Why so much war? Why so many different religions? Why so much crime and agony? Why do you have power issues? Why are you facing such an insecure future? Where is God? Is he truly there? Is he asleep?

God is not what you may think it is. For many of you reading these pages, you will grasp the concepts behind these words. However, there are many others who do not want to open their mind to this understanding because it is too difficult after years of believing in one Creator, that somehow that One Creator is not as what they believed it to be.

I will give you a lesson on your spirituality and on your spiritual life. Many truth seekers understand these lessons and many are opening to these words.

You and us, we all come from the same light. We have different purposes. You have come here as the Family of Light to this earth plane, which you call your home, because you desire to bring it back to perfection in the way it was originally.

Each time you come to your plane, you struggle in these dense energies to remember who you are in the light and to remember why you came here. What is your higher purpose? In these dense energies earth is presenting, you feel the pain of the people. The pain and the waves of fears engulfing upon your planet makes you forget why you came here.

We, Pleiadians, also evolve and come back to our planetary systems in different incarnations. We come because we desire to evolve into greatness. We do not have the pain and the fear you have, hence we remember who we were in the light and we do not suffer with memory loss as you do.

All your star brothers and sisters in light, work hard to create harmony in light because we all desire to evolve higher. Evolution will always be the purpose of all that is around you in existence.

In the realms of light, our true home, there is no confusion and misery. We do not discuss our personal fears because there are none. We are uplifting to each other and we learn to create greatness in our spiritual lives. We make plans and discuss them together. We discuss our journeys together and learn much from each other. We enjoy our spiritual lives.

Therefore, can you not see that although you may live on a different dimensional system than us, we all come from the same place although it may be differently organized?

Bottom line, we are all connected and we all desire the same, that is evolution and ridding the universe from fear.

Who are your creators? Is there one creator? You had many creators. Many scientists on different levels live in the universe. Each one has a different level of understanding and growth.

You come from the stars.

Is there one God?

There exists a Sovereign Light, the Sovereign Will. However, this Sovereign One delegates creation to allow expansion on all levels to take place. It is all about learning. The Great One, is All Intelligence, All Knowing, All Omniscient, Alpha and Omega. The Great Sovereign Being is Pure Energy Force, pure love and pure creation.

When universes are born, many Creators or high Elders who are star beings borrow the field of creative energy to build and create universes and species. We trust you understand a little about the process of creation now.

A Komo Ha Halima, I AM Halisarius, Pleiadian Chief Leader. I promised you I would come to call you back to the love consciousness.

Divine Creator of All of Existence

Divine Creator of All of Existence,

desired to expand,

desired to understand,

greater self,

greater exploration,

greater awareness,

greater love,

to open to a new creation,

of greater light within itself,

to grow,

to expand,

to discover,

to evolve,

to discover greater love,

greater power,

to bring all creation,

to greater stages,

of eternal love.

A Komo Ha Halima

Greetings, I AM Halisarius,

Pleiadian Chief Commander & Chief Leader,

Great Leader of the Galactic Federation of Light Society.

Part 86: The sacredness of Earth

It is a great honor to be present with you at this time. We are sending much of our love to you and much of our greetings to you.

Earth is a sacred ground. Earth is a jewel of creation. Your earth is filled with treasures from the stars. Your earth is sacred to us.

This is because the age old question will be answered on your planet.

After the accusation and the many threats, the White Brotherhood discussed the issues with us and we came to a universal agreement.

When we come to a universal agreement, this must be followed through, even for the ones who decide they do not desire this way.

It was brought before the ones who were the rebels. Between the times of meetings their armies had become much bigger. Now they were in the millions. Since their first approach in front of the Ancient Holy Brothers in Light, others had come to believe in them and took their side, truly believing they were in the right.

How difficult it was for us as star beings in the light to see this great division taking place. Never before in history of the Universe had division existed, perhaps on a small scale, but not on this grand level.

How rebellious they were. However, even with the rebellious attitude they still had to show respect before the Almighty Brothers. Disrespect is not taken well and could be a reason for imprisonment.

Imprisonment you ask? Yes, there are also spiritual prisons for those who are rebellious and do not show respect and will not listen. They are bound and they cannot do anything. It is a dark place and I would not encourage anyone to visit this place.

Your next question would be; why were they not imprisoned when they raised these issues?

We also had the same challenge. We also wanted this very much. How quickly peace would have been restored. How quickly the powers would have been restored.

However, the Great Sacred White Brotherhood, their knowledge is supreme. They know the future. They can understand the issues far greater than we can. They can foretell the future with such accuracy. They knew that imprisoning would not solve the issue. Others would continue to battle against light and the light did not desire this. Light wanted to prove the point that all ownership goes to the One who created all of Life.

Let us go into the scene and observe what happened.

Here we have the rebellious ones, claiming to be in the power, standing in front of the Great Sacred White Brotherhood. Twenty four Elders stood before them.

Many records of their conversations were written and recorded in history to be saved as an echo into all the universal history of both past and into the future so this issue would never be raised again.

The Great Sacred White Brotherhood asked them not to speak and to stay silent. These following words are in our records:

'You have challenged the greatest powers in the Universal Light. You have challenged the Great Power of The One who created all of Light and Life. You have challenged the entire force of the Brotherhood of the Universal Supreme Powers.

'We understand your desires. We have come together with an agreement and you must take this agreement. If you do not we will imprison you now and you will never be able to be free again.'

Silence in the courtroom.

The rebels looked up at the Great Sacred White Brotherhood and said, 'Speak please.'

The Great Elders continued to speak:

'We will give you an opportunity to find your answers. We will allow you to work with your ways to help you discover whether you are right or whether you are wrong.

'If however, you are found in the wrong, you must surrender all your weapons of destruction. You will be placed on your planets with Angels holding you back on those planets and you will not enter the atmosphere of another star existence until your hearts are in light. Until you have changed your ways.

'If we are found wrong and light is not found and you do indeed place such a darkness of destruction into the hearts, you will have the other planets.

'You will be allowed to play your part for a number of years and then we will bring light back. Let the people choose. Let the hearts be awakened. Let the battle of Light and Dark begin. May the glory of the Great Light forever be. May all the glory and the power return to the One who Created us All. We will win. You will fall in front of us. Know this.'

The rebels did not favor the decision. They respected the Great Light and knew the power of the Great Light but could not refuse it.

What did this decision mean? They were given a planet. This planet was called Earth and light beings would be placed upon the earth to bring her light. We (as star beings) were free to bring light before the darkness became evident, before the Great Battle began.

This is why we often refer to the earth as the precious jewel where the great battle is taking place, the planet where all our precious records are found. Your star friends came to earth and each placed a gift into earth, to help you remember the Great Light.

Light brothers and sisters desired to come to earth and play roles to bring light to earth to help you remember your light.

When the darkness began, many of you as the Family of Light decided to come back over and over again in different incarnations to fight darkness. You were brave and strong.

You were never on your own. We also gave you many gifts of light to carry you through. Although the battle was hard, it was never too much for the lovers of light.

The beings of darkness, claiming to be your masters, did everything in their power to make you fall hard. They changed your DNA, they gave you incredible fear, they placed leaders upon your earth and used them with their mind control, they created battles and religions. They have done much harm.

The net they placed around your earth stopped anyone from reaching the Great Light for a long time. When teachers came to the earth to show light, such as Jesus, they were tortured and stopped by leaders who were controlled by these dark energies.

You may say it is not fair that you are involved in a battle you did not agree on.

Greetings, I AM Halisarius, your teacher and Pleiadian Leader. I am here to call the Star Beings of Love back to the planets of love. Can you see you come from the stars?

The earth, a precious jewel

The earth,

A precious jewel,

created with the greatest love,

created with the greatest secrets,

of the universe,

holding great importance,

to all of creation.

Though it looks small,

in the greater spaces,

it is not small with secrets,

with its beauty,

for it is from the great love.

Let all suffering be gone,

let light live forever upon it,

let light shine within the hearts,

of all the people.

Let it Shine,

forever.

A Komo Ha Halima

Greetings, I AM Halisarius,

Pleiadian Chief Commander & Chief Leader,

Great Leader of the Galactic Federation of Light Society.

Part 87: Is Dark still working against Light?

We wonder how your reaction will be? Many of you will be happy because you can understand why there is trouble on your planet and how the pieces fit in together. They fit your world do they not? Why else would the anger and the hatred exist? Why else would a brother turn against his mother, or his sister? Their energies, of the rebellious ones, exist everywhere.

Make no mistake. These beings do not like the Great Light. They will fight against the Great Light, as they have over a very long time. Who else was behind the so called 'witch hunts?' Many of you are still very frightened of sharing your gifts because you have deep memories of being killed, tortured and persecuted.

Could it be true there are darker forces working against the Great Light on your planet?

Many of you know the answers. Many of you have always believed it is the work of Satan.

It is true, these beings have satanic energies. They have dark, angry, revengeful energies, since 'their time is very short.'

However, they are not truly satanic, or demons. Like we have said in previous pages in this book, they will be healed in the Great Light. They have become lost and do not remember their true heritage of love.

Do not be angry with them because it will only give them more power.

This is why they have become strong on your planet because of the anger and the hate on your planet. Look at the wars and the killings. Look at the anger against another. Look at the rebellion and the protesting and the fighting among you.

You may here ask me, 'Is it not normal for us as human beings to do this? Is our behavior not normal?'

We will answer this for you and say please, 'Awaken.'

Your natural state is love. You understand love as you have it within you to awaken to the love. When you look at your beauty on your earth, you feel the presence of peace and love. Is this not within your heart then?

No person on your planet is truly 'evil.' Again you may quote me people who have killed many and have had evil plans.

We, as your brothers and sisters on the Pleiadian Realms of light will say this to you dear ones. 'Please let go of your pain, as your pain will add more fuel and more power to darkness. Can you not see people have been used by these beings to do all these things? Can you not see the mind control, the fear these beings have placed within your hearts? Can you not see your true nature of love?'

Your people are in deep pain and fear. We will help you to heal this pain and fear and allow you to bring the love back into your hearts. However, you must desire this first.

We will help you, including the multitude of the heavenly Great Light Beings of Love, to heal within yourselves, to heal your cellular memory and awaken you to truth within yourselves.

This pain you have carried and still have, are pains of illusions. These are not your own energies for they have been created by other beings. These rebels and vultures have placed them within the hearts of men who were angry. When a person on your plane is angry it becomes easy for them to be manipulated by these dark beings of great defiance.

Why? Because when one is in fear and anger, one becomes weak energetically. Their energy can be pulled away from them towards these beings. They are eating you energetically. You are starving energetically.

Please awaken.

Can you change your planetary situation? Is there hope?

Certainly. Why do you think we are here to help awaken you? Why do you think your Archangels, Divine Beings, and beings on higher dimensions have been placing light for you and holding higher spaces for your growth and healing?

We know who you are. We know the strength within you. The Holy Ancient White Brotherhood did not give this challenge without having confidence in you first. They knew you could do it and bring back the harmony on your planet and thus bring back the harmony in our universe in its entirety.

How happy we are to know you will do this. Many light workers are awakening and have already awakened.

Bring in light and anchor it down. Teach others how to live in the love for the flow of love will awaken them. Bring in the greatness and the teachings of light.

Much will be revealed to you in the near future.

You will not be afraid anymore when these beings of darkness have gone. You will not be angry anymore. You will not hunger anymore, for then the harmony will return to your planet.

Greetings, I AM Halisarius, Pleiadian Leader. Our task is to guide you home. We promised to parent all who desired to listen to the love flows.

Your Sacred Heart

Your Sacred Heart,

has a sacred doorway,

to your deeper knowledge,

to your greater understanding,

to your great answers to your questions,

to your challenges,

within your world.

May your hearts awaken together,

to stand together,

united as one.

Open your hearts together,

to the Great Love.

Invite us into your hearts,

to open more of your love,

and then all your greatness,

will return to you,

with eternal love, power,

and wisdom.

A Komo Ha Halima

Greetings, I AM Halisarius,

Pleiadian Chief Commander & Chief Leader,

Great Leader of the Galactic Federation of Light Society.

Part 88: Your powerful secret within you

We are wondering how you are taking all this information? This information is ancient. It is not new. We are helping you to remember who you are.

All through our time together in this book, we have helped you to understand more about who we are as your Pleiadian friends. We have given you the insight to our life and we have also given you great insight to your history and how you play a great part in your history. We also gave you the insight to the 'Great Restoration of Consciousness.'

We ask you to leave these matters in the hands of the Divine Beings who we trust in. We ask you also to place your trust in them. They are working hard for you at this very moment to create higher ways of growth.

We also ask you to understand that not all people on your earth require change before these beings lose their control on your planet.

Please listen very carefully to this message and take it within your heart, your Sacred Heart of Great Love.

You have an ancient secret within you. We have already allowed you to discover this secret within the pages of this book. However, I will share it with you once again.

You have a powerful secret within you. When you understand it and allow it to be revealed, these rebellious beings will have lost their war.

Your Sacred Heart has a deep connection to each other and to the Greatest Source of Power in existence. When your Sacred Heart awakens together in groups, you are doing much to allow the rebels to pack up and go home. Please understand this within your third eye, which is a portal to higher dimensions and understanding.

Your third eye and your Sacred Heart are connected. When you open both centers your love for who you are becomes great. Imagine if a group did this together and another group also did this and many groups grew because they could understand these exercises. How much love would be anchored down on your planet?

Your world has lacked love and light for hundreds of thousands of years. It was dense in its energies. Light found it hard to penetrate because of the dark net with many messages of confusion within it.

Light became stronger when the hearts of people opened. You reached out to light. You called out to light first. Light responded and broke through this thick, vast net. The more light came to your planet, the greater the awakening of the hearts.

Please understand from this message the power you have within you. You open up to the great love within you through your Sacred Hearts. Archangels can only help you when your Sacred Heart calls out to light, for then light from the Greatness of all of existence responds to your Sacred Heart.

Do not underestimate these dark beings. When light awakens within the people they will aim to bring darkness back. After all, your fear and anger means their life. They do not desire to be forced to a life filled with light.

Can you understand their anger and desire for revenge?

You do not need to be afraid for they cannot do anything to you any longer. They have already lost the battle energetically. Their confusion will remain still with you for a while.

Keep releasing your fear to the Angels.

Understand you will bring change. Your hearts will become like fires burning, desiring to open to greater portals within you.

When you come together as one, honor each other and shine your Sacred Centers of your spiritual hearts towards each other. Feel only love flowing through you. Do it together in a group and be in that space for a while. Then visualize your third eyes awakening to light above you. As you join your Sacred Hearts together and visualize your third eye being in light above, you are shining your hearts to light.

A Komo Ha Halima, I AM Halisarius, Pleiadian Chief Leader. I promised you I would come to call you back to the love consciousness.

A Komo Ha Halima

Greetings, I AM Halisarius,

Pleiadian Chief Commander & Chief Leader,

Great Leader of the Galactic Federation of Light Society.

Part 89: Conclusion from Halisarius, Chief Pleiadian Leader, Leader on the Galactic Federations of Light

Before concluding these pages of love from my being, Halisarius, I asked Suzanna to make the following addition to the original pages.

As many of you know, I, Halisarius, am a great leader of the Galactic Federations of Light Society. I, Halisarius, am greatly blessing all who desire to become part of the Great Family of Light.

In 2014, when I asked Suzanna to sit with me to write this book for you, she did not know Caeayaron was working with her.

After this book was written, Caeayaron approached her and she began to understand her greater purpose as a Light Grid Programmer of Caeayaron, and also a Star Grid Programmer for the Galactic Federations of Light.

You are now being called by Caeayaron to come to the great healings taking place at this time; to the Divine Pineal Gland Activations which bring you back into your ancient love codes, to allow you to stand in the great love. We, as Star Beings in the great love, are here applauding each person upon your earth who becomes activated as they are then released from the limitation, and grow towards their greater love consciousness.

To bring peace and love to your plane, Caeayaron is gifting all who become activated with a stronger energy system, to allow you to awaken to greater love flows. Also, we as Star Beings, are then able to create greater healing frequencies within you, to allow you to come into your greater star gifts.

We, as Star Beings of the Great Love, say; 'The time has arrived for the people to awaken. The time has arrived for the greater path to become clearer. We celebrate the times of the light. We celebrate the great healings. We celebrate your return to the great love.'

This is all that is required at this moment. We will teach you much about how to heal your flows within yourselves to bring back unity upon your planet.

In this book we have discussed much with you. How much have you taken in and enjoyed? How much have you understood to be your stories of truth?

During this time together, we have given you transmissions for your cellular memory to awaken. We desire to bring you to higher portals of light and understanding.

Our prayers are with you. Our Sacred Hearts are with you. Our love is with you. Our higher visions of seeing you awaken, as a race, are with you.

We are working solidly with you by your side. You are not alone in this battle for we are also working with you. You have each other and if only a small number of your total population awaken to your Sacred Hearts, these beings of defiance will soon be gone.

Remember, they hate light. Do not be angry with them for the anger feeds them. Forgive and stay in the forgiveness.

Do not fight anymore with each other. Resolve to stay peaceful. When you are jealous, understand how love will heal.

We have enjoyed bringing you these messages and stories. We have enjoyed bringing you light.

We wish you well on your journeys of healing. We will speak to you again with more healing books in the near future, allowing you to discover your greater self.

Until then;

A Komo Ha Halima, Greetings, from myself and our Pleiadian race, I AM Halisarius, your Teacher, your Guide, Pleiadian Chief Leader for our Pleiadian people and a Chief Advisor on the Galactic Federation of Light Society. I AM Chief Commander on the Galactic Federation of Light Society Bodies.

Printed in Great Britain
by Amazon

54427738R00165